# First World War
### and Army of Occupation
# War Diary
### France, Belgium and Germany

5 CAVALRY DIVISION
Divisional Troops
17 Brigade Royal Horse Artillery
1 January 1917 - 31 March 1918

WO95/1163/1

The Naval & Military Press Ltd
www.nmarchive.com
**Published in association with The National Archives**

Published by

## The Naval & Military Press Ltd

Unit 10 Ridgewood Industrial Park,

Uckfield, East Sussex,

TN22 5QE England

Tel: +44 (0) 1825 749494

www.naval-military-press.com

www.nmarchive.com

*This diary has been reprinted in facsimile from the original. Any imperfections are inevitably reproduced and the quality may fall short of modern type and cartographic standards.*

© **Crown Copyright**
**Images reproduced by permission of The National Archives, London, England, 2015.**

# Contents

| Document type | Place/Title | Date From | Date To |
|---|---|---|---|
| Heading | WO95/1163/1 | | |
| Heading | 17th Bde., R.H.A. Jan 1917-Mar 1918 | | |
| Heading | War Diary of 2nd Indian R.H.A. Brigade. From 1st January 1917 To 31st January 1917 | | |
| War Diary | Incheville | 01/01/1917 | 31/01/1917 |
| War Diary | Beauchamps Incheville Oust Mares Pont at Marais | 05/02/1917 | 26/02/1917 |
| War Diary | Cerisy | 01/04/1917 | 01/04/1917 |
| War Diary | Villers Bretonneux | 01/04/1917 | 01/04/1917 |
| War Diary | Bayonvillers | 01/04/1917 | 01/04/1917 |
| War Diary | La Motte | 01/04/1917 | 01/04/1917 |
| War Diary | Cappy | 01/04/1917 | 01/04/1917 |
| War Diary | (Canal Camp) No 57 | 13/04/1917 | 14/04/1917 |
| War Diary | Guizancourt Mr Trefcon Mr Caulxincourt Falvy | 16/04/1917 | 16/04/1917 |
| War Diary | Falvy | 21/04/1917 | 21/04/1917 |
| War Diary | Trefcon | 23/04/1917 | 23/04/1917 |
| War Diary | Caulaincourt | 23/04/1917 | 23/04/1917 |
| War Diary | Guizancourt | 25/04/1917 | 26/04/1917 |
| War Diary | Guizancourt & Neighbourhood | 01/05/1917 | 08/05/1917 |
| War Diary | Hamelet | 09/05/1917 | 09/05/1917 |
| War Diary | Guizancourt | 10/05/1917 | 14/05/1917 |
| War Diary | Nobescourt Farm | 15/05/1917 | 31/05/1917 |
| Operation(al) Order(s) | 5th. Cavalry Divisional Artillery Operation Order No. 4 | 25/05/1917 | 25/05/1917 |
| Miscellaneous | 5th Cavalry Divisional Artillery Operation Order No. 4 | | |
| Miscellaneous | Barrage Table 28th. H.A. Group To Accompany 5th. Cavalry Divisional Artillery O.O. No. 4 | | |
| Miscellaneous | 5th Cavalry Divisional Artillery. | | |
| War Diary | Nobescourt Farm Divnl H.Q | 01/06/1917 | 13/06/1917 |
| War Diary | Neghtes | 16/06/1917 | 29/06/1917 |
| Operation(al) Order(s) | 5th. Cavalry Divisional Artillery Operation Order No. 5 | 01/06/1917 | 01/06/1917 |
| Miscellaneous | Table "A" To Accompany 5th. Cav. Divn. Arty. Operation Order No. 5 | | |
| Miscellaneous | Table "B" To Accompany 5th. Cav. Divn. Artillery Operation Order No. 5 | | |
| Operation(al) Order(s) | 5th. Cavalry Divisional Artillery Operation Order No. 6 | 10/06/1917 | 10/06/1917 |
| Operation(al) Order(s) | 5th Cavalry Divisional Artillery O.O. No. 7 | 12/06/1917 | 12/06/1917 |
| Miscellaneous | 5th. Cavalry Divisional Artillery Barrage Table To Accompany Operation Order No.7 | | |
| Miscellaneous | Headquarters, 5th. Cav. Divn. Arty. | 12/06/1917 | 12/06/1917 |
| Operation(al) Order(s) | 5th, Cavalry Divisional Artillery Operation Order No. 8 | 14/06/1917 | 14/06/1917 |
| Operation(al) Order(s) | 5th, Cavalry Divisional Artillery O.O. No.9 | 16/06/1917 | 16/06/1917 |
| Miscellaneous | 5th. Cavalry Divisional Artillery.barrage Table To Accompany Operation Order No. 9 | | |
| Operation(al) Order(s) | 5th. Cavalry Divisional Artillery O.O. No. 10 | 21/06/1917 | 21/06/1917 |
| Operation(al) Order(s) | 5th. Cavalry Divisional Artillery O.O. No. 11 | 22/06/1917 | 22/06/1917 |
| Operation(al) Order(s) | 5th. Cavalry Divisional Artillery O.O. No. 12 | 26/06/1917 | 26/06/1917 |
| Miscellaneous | 5th. Cavalry Divisional Artillery Instructions No. 1 | 25/06/1917 | 25/06/1917 |
| Miscellaneous | 5th. Cavalry Divisional Artillery Instructions No. 2 | 26/06/1917 | 26/06/1917 |
| Miscellaneous | 5th, Cavalry Divisional Artillery Instructions No. 3 | 29/06/1917 | 29/06/1917 |
| War Diary | Nobescourt Farm | 01/07/1917 | 10/07/1917 |
| War Diary | Nobescourt Farm & Bouvincourt | 10/07/1917 | 11/07/1917 |

| | | | |
|---|---|---|---|
| War Diary | Bouvincourt | 12/07/1917 | 15/07/1917 |
| War Diary | Cappy | 15/07/1917 | 15/07/1917 |
| War Diary | Heilly Mericourt. | 16/07/1917 | 16/07/1917 |
| War Diary | Orville Amplier Authville | 17/07/1917 | 17/07/1917 |
| War Diary | St Pol | 18/07/1917 | 27/07/1917 |
| War Diary | Gauchin Legal | 28/07/1917 | 28/07/1917 |
| War Diary | Corons D'aix | 29/07/1917 | 31/07/1917 |
| Miscellaneous | C. R. H. A. 5th, Cav Div. | 29/06/1917 | 29/06/1917 |
| Miscellaneous | 17th Bde R. H. A. | 09/07/1917 | 09/07/1917 |
| Operation(al) Order(s) | 5th. Cavalry Divisional Artillery Operation Order No. 16 | 07/07/1917 | 07/07/1917 |
| Miscellaneous | Table of Barrages To Accompany 5th. Cavalry Div"l Artillery O.O. No. 16 | | |
| Operation(al) Order(s) | 5th. Cavalry Divisional Artillery Operation Order No. 17 | 09/07/1917 | 09/07/1917 |
| Miscellaneous | 5th, Cavalry Divisional Artillery Relief Table Issued With Operation Order No. 17 | | |
| War Diary | Corons D'aix | 01/08/1917 | 19/08/1917 |
| War Diary | Lievin & Neighbourhood | 20/08/1917 | 31/08/1917 |
| War Diary | Lievin | 01/09/1917 | 07/09/1917 |
| War Diary | Corons D'aix | 07/09/1917 | 08/09/1917 |
| War Diary | Ourton | 09/09/1917 | 09/09/1917 |
| War Diary | Bergueneuse & Billets | 10/09/1917 | 15/09/1917 |
| War Diary | Wavrans | 16/09/1917 | 19/09/1917 |
| War Diary | In billets | 01/08/1917 | 30/08/1917 |
| War Diary | Bergueneuse Hestrus Gubbys & Neuville Farm | 01/10/1917 | 01/10/1917 |
| War Diary | Hestrus | 02/10/1917 | 02/10/1917 |
| War Diary | Same Area | 03/10/1917 | 06/10/1917 |
| War Diary | Steenbecque | 07/10/1917 | 07/10/1917 |
| War Diary | Poperinghe Area | 08/10/1917 | 09/10/1917 |
| War Diary | Same Area | 10/10/1917 | 14/10/1917 |
| War Diary | Renescure | 15/10/1917 | 15/10/1917 |
| War Diary | Bout De La Ville | 16/10/1917 | 16/10/1917 |
| War Diary | Planques Area | 17/10/1917 | 19/10/1917 |
| War Diary | Iame Area | 20/10/1917 | 31/10/1917 |
| War Diary | Planques Area | 01/11/1917 | 03/11/1917 |
| War Diary | Fruges | 05/11/1917 | 05/11/1917 |
| War Diary | Planques | 06/11/1917 | 10/11/1917 |
| War Diary | Mezerolles | 11/11/1917 | 11/11/1917 |
| War Diary | Querrieu | 12/11/1917 | 12/11/1917 |
| War Diary | Cappy | 13/11/1917 | 13/11/1917 |
| War Diary | Bouvincourt | 14/11/1917 | 20/11/1917 |
| War Diary | Between Villers-Pluich And Marcoing | 21/11/1917 | 22/11/1917 |
| War Diary | Equancourt | 23/11/1917 | 24/11/1917 |
| War Diary | Suzanne | 26/11/1917 | 27/11/1917 |
| War Diary | Monchy Lagache | 28/11/1917 | 30/12/1917 |
| War Diary | Near Vendelles | 01/01/1918 | 19/02/1918 |
| War Diary | Monohy Lagache | 21/02/1918 | 28/02/1918 |
| War Diary | Bouvincourt | 01/03/1918 | 14/03/1918 |
| War Diary | Monchy Lagache | 15/03/1918 | 22/03/1918 |
| War Diary | Ennemain | 23/03/1918 | 23/03/1918 |
| War Diary | Chaulnes | 24/03/1918 | 25/03/1918 |
| War Diary | Rosiere Les Santerre | 25/03/1918 | 26/03/1918 |
| War Diary | Demuin | 26/03/1918 | 28/03/1918 |
| War Diary | Castrel To Cottench | 29/03/1918 | 29/03/1918 |
| War Diary | Domart Boves | 30/03/1918 | 30/03/1918 |

| | | | |
|---|---|---|---|
| War Diary | Cottenchy | 31/03/1918 | 31/03/1918 |
| Miscellaneous | Eagle Troop R H A 21/29 3 18 | | |
| Miscellaneous | On The Part Taken By The Eagle Troop R.H.A. In The Fighting From March 21st To 29th Inclusive. | | |

WO 95/11631

# 1917-1918
## 5TH CAVALRY DIVISION

17TH BDE., R.H.A.

JAN 1917 - MAR 1918

SERIAL NO. 295

# Confidential

## War Diary

of

2nd INDIAN R.H.A. BRIGADE.

FROM 1st January 1917. TO 31st January 1917.

**WAR DIARY** ◦ 2nd Bn R.W.F Regt

or

**INTELLIGENCE SUMMARY.** ◦ Vol IX

Army Form C. 2118.

*(Erase heading not required.)*

| Place | Date | Hour | Summary of Events and Information | Remarks and references to Appendices |
|---|---|---|---|---|
| INCHEVILLE | Jan 1st | | Brigade Heavy Transport Training | |
| " | 2nd | | Lieut J.A. Foster 24th appointed to 2nd Inst Regt 3/4 | |
| " | 3rd to 20th | | Usual Routine | |
| | 21st | | 2/Lieut J.S. Culliver N. Patrey, L.H. attached Tank Coplin Recce Coplin A.M. Morten to Guards Div Coly. 20.12.16 | |
| | 22nd to 31st | | Usual Routine. Musketry Training | |

W.H. [signature]
2/Lieut PPO
for O/C 2nd Batt. R.W.F. Bde

Army Form C. 2118.

# WAR DIARY
## or
## INTELLIGENCE SUMMARY

*(Erase heading not required.)*

17th R.H.A. Brigade. — February.  Vol X

| Place | Date | Hour | Summary of Events and Information | Remarks and references to Appendices |
|---|---|---|---|---|
| BEAUCHAMPS INCHEVILLE OUST MAREST PONT of MARAIS | | | In rest billets | |
| | 5.2.17 6.2.17 | | Guns of the Brigade overhauled, and redistributed according to wear. 2/Lt. A. N. Dickson joined the brigade on appointment to RHA from 2/Lieut. 3rd Division 2/Lt. W. C. TOWELL M.C. " " | |
| | 14.2.17 | | 2/Lt Dickson posted to X Battery, 2/Lt Towell to N Battery Inspection of the Brigade by the Division Commander. | |
| | 14.2.17 | | Captain D. S. Anderson to England to attend course at Overseas Artillery School. | |
| | 22.2.17 | | Captain Riley left the Brigade on appointment to the command of 36th Divn Am. Col. | |
| | 23.2.17 | | 2/Lts Towell & Dickson to R.H.A. School Cavalry Corps to attend 4th R.H.A. Course. | |
| | 26.2.17 | | 2/Lt Hellings joined the brigade from the base, and was posted to M. Bry. Usual routine & Battery training. | |

C. A. Buchan? Major
for Lt Col Cmdg 17th R.H.A. Bde.

# WAR DIARY or INTELLIGENCE SUMMARY

Army Form C. 2118.

(Erase heading not required.)

Instructions regarding War Diaries and Intelligence Summaries are contained in F. S. Regs., Part II. and the Staff Manual respectively. Title Pages will be prepared in manuscript.

Vol 12

*Africa* [?] ............ *Anti-Aircraft* ... N x Batteries ...
................................. 17th Bty. HQrs. Brigade...

| Place | Date | Hour | Summary of Events and Information | Remarks and references to Appendices |
|---|---|---|---|---|
| BRAY | April | | Brigade in rest billets in but forward area. | |
| CERISY. | 1.4.17 | | HQrs moved forward to taken Bretonneux and moved to Bayonvillers. | |
| VILLERS BRETONNEUX | 5 " | | | |
| BAYONVILLERS | " | | HQrs. with Divnl. HQrs. | |
| LAMOTTE. | " | | N Battery & L x in Anmn. Col. | |
| " | " | | X ............ and X x in Anmn. Col. } Battery training in shooting work with aeroplanes, and staff rides for officers. | |
| CAPPY | " | | | |
| (small camp no.57) | 13.4.17 | | Near Amiens, Corbie. | |
| " | 9.4.17 | | British prisoner on 11th Army front front reports L.Y. Army massed breaking conditions most unfavourable xxxxx anxious. | |
| " | 14.4.17 | | Orders received to move on 12.4.17 to Cavalier 11.0 pm | |
| " | 14.4.17 | | Division transported left at 7.30 am. Convoy Lieut. Hemans to BRIG. Bde BRIGADE to BRIGADE to Lieut & Hurly at headquarters. | |
| Bde QRs GUIZANCOURT. | | | WIG Brd. Hd Qrs. to Lieut & Hurly at headquarters | |
| Mons CHILLINCOURT. | | | N Battery & L x | |
| PALVY. | 16.4.17 | | Bdes Arrives Col. ......... new orders strength | |

Army Form C. 2118.

# WAR DIARY
## or
## INTELLIGENCE SUMMARY
(Erase heading not required.)

| Place | Date | Hour | Summary of Events and Information | Remarks and references to Appendices |
|---|---|---|---|---|
| FALVY | 21.4.17 | 5.8pm | Infantry & HE fire Annan Column h/ FSE Dn & P3h10 | |
| TREFCON | 23.4.17 | Noon | Infantry & N. Bolonn Coln | |
| | | Noon | B FSC Div in P3h10 | |
| BAULAINCOURT | " | Noon | x | |
| BUZANCOURT | 25.4.17 | 5.15am | Infantry & Rather Bolc in P3h10 h/ FSC Dn | |
| | | | 2/c Mourgenes RFA Outpost (nearby Officer & 65 other ranks) Rah | |
| " | 30.4.17 | | Battery training Work with Keroplanes | |

P.A. Newton
V/C RFA
Adjt. 2nd Bde RFA

Army Form C. 2118.

Vol XIII

# WAR DIARY
## or
## INTELLIGENCE SUMMARY

May. – Rest billets in forward area.
17" R.H.A. Brigade.

(Erase heading not required.)

| Place | Date May | Hour | Summary of Events and Information | Remarks and references to Appendices |
|---|---|---|---|---|
| GUIZANCOURT & neighbourhood | 1st | 10:30 am | Inspection of 17" Bde RHA, RCHA Bde. by Gen. Seligman. Cdr. RHA. Cav. Corps. | |
| – do – | 1st–6th | – | | |
| | 7th | – | Battery training. | |
| – do – | 8th | – | Brigade marched to bivouacs near HAMELET under orders of III d Corps and attached to 59th Division. | |
| HAMELET | 9th | – | Reconnoitred battery positions – operation cancelled. | |
| GUIZANCOURT | 10th | – | Returned to original bivouacs. | |
| – do – | 10th–13th | – | Battery training. | |
| – do – | 14th | – | Q & U Batteries RHA. arrive, and come under orders of Lt. Col. Stirling, CRHA 5th Cav Div. | |
| – do – | 14th | – | Brigade Hd. Qrs. moved from GUIZANCOURT to NOBESCOURT FARM. Cavalry take over a portion of the line held by 59th Div. | |
| NOBESCOURT FARM. | 15th | – | I Xn. from Q & U. went into action on 35th Div. front under orders of CRA. 35th Div. | |
| – do – | 16th | – | Remainder of Q & U go into action. | |
| – do – | 17th | – | I Xn. of N & X batteries RHA and of A & B batteries RCHA go into action relieving a corresponding number of X n's of 55th Div. artillery. 3 Staff Sergts RCHA Bde HQrs. accidentally wounded by explosion of bomb. | |

# WAR DIARY or INTELLIGENCE SUMMARY

Army Form C. 2118.

| Place | Date | Hour | Summary of Events and Information | Remarks and references to Appendices |
|---|---|---|---|---|
| NOBESCOURT | 18th | | Remainder of 118th RHA Batteries form in Station. | |
| do | 19th | | Divisional Arty. organised in 3 sub-sectors. Artillery organising in 2 groups. — Right Group consisting of 6 RHA Batteries under OC. 16th Bde. RHA. covering the southern & centre sub. sectors. Left Group consisting of 25th Bde. RFA and under orders HQR/Arty 3rd Cav. Divn, covering the northern sub-sector. Head Qrs. 15th Bde. RHA & RCHA combined to form Hd. Qrs. RA. 3rd Cav. Divn. CRA:- Col. W. Starling DSO GMK. — Lt Col. W.P. Elkins RCHA acting as Bde Major R.A. | |
| do | 20th | | } Registration by subsections. | |
| do | 21st | | | |
| do | 22nd | | 63. Battery RCHA. move forward to a more advanced position. | |
| do | 23rd | | Weekly Conference of Artillery Reconnaissance officers. | |
| do | 24th | | | |
| do | 25th | | Normal firing — some registration. | |

## WAR DIARY or INTELLIGENCE SUMMARY

Army Form C. 2118.

(3.)

| Place | Date | Hour | Summary of Events and Information | Remarks and references to Appendices |
|---|---|---|---|---|
| NOEUX LES MINES | 26th/27th | 2.15 am | Canadian Cav. Bde. sterling right, on District, extracted an enemy work called FISHER'S CRATER, supported by artillery fire. Our batteries with assistance from hr Corps Heavy Artillery fired from 2.15 am to 2.45 am, when the raiding party returned. The enemy arm thought to have suffered heavy casualties from our artillery fire. — 18 prisoners taken, our casualties 1 K. & 2 wounded. Artillery orders & location of batteries & [guns?] attached. | Trench Sheet 62.B.S.W. 1:20,000 French Div. on right  M 3 E.O.S. |
|  | 27th | — | Divnl. Hd. Qrs. Inverss inspected by G.O.C. | |
|  | 28th | — | 2/ Tod. Joined the Brigade from England & posted to "X" Battery R.H.A. | |
|  | 29th | — | Support line of MP. & W. sector heavily shelled, destroying | |
|  | 30th | — | our cookhouse. Steps [taken?] by the intervention of our Counter Battery Group. | |
|  | 31st | — | No hostile counter battery work directed against our Interior. No casualties. | |

G.C. Preston Lt Col Cmdg R.H.A. Bde. H.Qrs. N.b.L.M. A.H.Q.

SECRET.

## 5th. CAVALRY DIVISIONAL ARTILLERY OPERATION ORDER No. 4

REFERENCE MAP
1/20,000 Sheet 4
BELLENGLISE 2nd. Edition.

Copy No.
25th. May 1917

1. A minor enterprise will be carried out by Canadian Cavalry Brigade on the night of the 26/27th. May at zero hour, with the intention of killing and capturing Germans in posts around Fishers Crater and Trees about G.32.d.9.1., and destroying their works.

2. Zero hour will be notified later.

3. At zero hour one troop advances on objective FISHERS CRATER from point about 200 yds. West of Crater.
   At the same time 2 troops advance on the trees about G.32.d.9.1. and Sunken Road East of it from a point about 20 yds. South of Eastern end of SOMERVILLE WOOD.

4. Both parties will be withdrawn clear of their objectives by zero + 30'.

5. Rockets (Red on the Right, Green on the Left) will be sent up in rear of both parties at zero + 30' to obviate possibility of any one being left behind.
   No attention will be paid by the Artillery to any rockets that may be sent up before zero + 30'.

6. Four Batteries 5th. Cavalry Divisional Artillery will co-operate in accordance with attached table.

7. Ammunition to be expended for this enterprise will be in excess of that already at guns, and present dump must be maintained.

8. Watches will be synchronized at Canadian Brigade Headquarters (VADENCOURT CHATEAU R.17.a.) at 7.30.p.m. 26-5-17.

9. 28th. H.A. Group will co-operate.

10. Acknowledge by wire.

Major R.C.H.A.
For 5th. Cavalry Divisional Art

Copy No. 1. Filed.
2. N Bty R.H.A.
3. X " R.H.A.
4. A. " R.C.H.A.
5. B. " R.C.H.A.
6. C. " 295th Bde.
7. R.H.A. Cav Corps.
8. 5th. Cav. Division.
9. Canadian Cavalry Bde.
10 tp 15 Spare.

| Battery | 1st. Objective | Time | Rate of Fire. | 2nd. Objective | Time | Rate of Fire. | 3rd. Objective | Time | Rate of Fire. | 4th. Objective | Time | Rate of Fire. | Total Rounds N.K | NK |
|---|---|---|---|---|---|---|---|---|---|---|---|---|---|---|
| A.R.C.H.A. 4 guns. | FISHER CRATER M.2.d.8.45. | Zero to +1' | 4 rds. per gun per min N.K | Ruins about M.3.c.25.6. | +1' to +3' | 4 rds. per gun per min. N | BELLENGLISE gunroad M.3.c.6.55. Barrage across road extending 40 yds. on either side | +3' to +6' | 3 rds. per gun per min. N | ST&HELENE TRENCH from M.3.d.2.85. to M.3.c.9.2. | +6' to +30' | 2 rds. per gun per min 50% N 50% NK | 184. | 115 |
| B.R.C.H.A. 4 guns. | ASCENSION VALLEY road from M.3.c.1.9. to G.33.c.1.15 | zero to +1' | 4 rds per gun per min N | ST&HELENE trench from M.3.c.9.2. to G.33.d.0.2. | +1' to +30' | 2 rds. per gun per min. 50% N 50% NK | | | | | | | 276. 132 | |

Total rounds 658 590 802

*Major R.C.H.A.*
For 5th. Cavalry Divisional Artillery.

TABLE showing Objectives, Times and Rate of Fire
to accompany
Artillery Operation Order No.4

5th. Cavalry Divisional

| Battery | 1st.Objective | Time | Rate of Fire | 2nd.Objective | Time | Rate of Fire | 3rd.Objective | Time | Rate of Fire | 4th.Objective | Time | Rate of Fire | Ammo. Rounds N / MX |
|---|---|---|---|---|---|---|---|---|---|---|---|---|---|
| No.R.H.A. 4 guns. | SQUARE COPSE G.33.d.0.6. & ST.HELENE trench from road G.33.d.0.2. to G.33.b.1.6. | ZERO to + 20 | 2 rds. per gun per minute 50% N. 50% MX | | | | | | | | | | 120 / 120 |
| 2 guns | ELEVEN TREES G.33.c.75.65. to G.33.a.6.05. | zero to + 30 | 2 rds. per gun per min. 50% N. 50% MX | | | | | | | | | | 60 / 60 |
| No.R.H.A. 4 guns. | Communication trench from junction M.5.a.95.95. to G.34.c.0.2. | zero to + 30 | 2 rds. per gun per min. 50% N. 50% MX | | | | | | | | | | 120 / 120 |
| 2 guns. | Bank between G.53.c.1.2. & G.33.c.75.65 | zero to + 1 | 4 rds. per gun per min. 50% N. 50% MX | Bank between G.33.c.5.35 & G.33.c.75.65 | + 1 to + 30 | 2 rds per gun per min. 50% N. 50% MX | | | | | | | 62 / 62 |

P.T.O.

## BARRAGE TABLE 29th.H.A.Group

### to accompany 5th.Cavalry Divisional Artillery O.O.No.4

### 109 SEIGE BATTERY

(a) Zero to zero+30 sec. on MAX WOOD about G.33.c.0.0. Shells to arrive at zero. 2 rounds per How.

(b) Zero+30 sec. to zero+30 min.
The above section will lift on to the bank and road crossing at G.33.c.75.60.
Rate of fire 1 round per How. per 2 min.

(c) One section to fire on the bank 100 yds. east of and parallel to MAX WOOD (on East side of road) from zero to zero+1 min.
Shells of first salvo to arrive at zero.
Ammunition allotted 5 rds. per How.

(d) Zero+1 min. to zero+30 min.
The section mentioned in (c) will lift to the bank and trench crossing at G.33.d.1.9.
Rate of fire 1 round per How. per 2 min.

### 40 SEIGE BATTERY

(a) One 6" How. to fire on trench and road crossing at H.3.d.0.9 from zero to zero+5 min.(first shell to arrive at zero) Rate of fire 1 rd. per min.
From zero+5 min. to zero+30 min. this How. will fire on the bend in the trench about G.34.c.0.1. Rate of fire 1 rd. per 2 min.

(b) Zero to zero+30 min.
One 6" How. to fire on the points where the communication trench crosses the road at H.3.b.0.6..
Rates of fire zero to zero+10 min. one rd. per min.
  "   "   "   zero+10 min. to zero+30 min. 1 rd. per 2 min.

(c) Zero to zero+30 min.
One 6" How. to fire on the bend in the trench about G.33.d.6.2.
Rate of fire 1 rd. per 2 min.

### 60 POUNDERS.

(a) One section to search and sweep head of the valley and road G.28.a. from zero+15 min. to zero+45 min.

(b) One section to search and sweep Valley E. of the wood in G.34.a. from zero+15 min. to zero+45 min.

Ammunition 80 rounds per section.

A Liaison Officer will be detailed by O.C. 29 H.A.G. for duty at Canadian Brigade Headquarters, and a special line will be laid.

Major R.G.H.A.
For 5th.Cav.Div. Artillery.

## 5th. Cavalry Divisional Artillery.

### LOCATION STATEMENT.

| Unit | Position. | | Wagon Lines. |
|---|---|---|---|
| 17th.Bde. R.H.A. Hdqrs. | 5th. Cav.Divn. H.Q.,R.A. | K.32.d.8.9. | |
| R.C.H.A. Bde. Hdqrs. | Advanced H.Q. Tel. Exchange | R.8.b.Central. | |

| | | |
|---|---|---|
| "N" Battery R.H.A. | R.4.c.3.3½. | W.II.a.and c. |
| "X" Battery R.H.A. | L.33.d.8.3. | W.3.b.9.6. |
| A Battery R.C.H.A. | R.16.b.4.7. | W.6.d. |
| B Battery R.C.H.A. | R.4.d.73.05. | W.6.d.Central. |
| A/295 Battery R.F.A. | L.21.c.7.5. | Hamelet. |
| D/298 Battery R.F.A. | R.II.a.17.72. | COUVIGNY FARM. |

| | |
|---|---|
| Ammunition Column | Q.32.c. |

| | |
|---|---|
| A.R.P. | Hancourt. |

"Heavies"

| | |
|---|---|
| 40th. Siege. (4-6" How.) | L.27.d.9.1. |
| 109th. Siege. (4-6" How.) | L.32.d.8.2. |
| 12th. Heavy. (4 60 pdrs) | L.26.c.6.6. |
| 120th. Heavy. (4-60 pdrs.) | L.13.c.6.3. |

Lieut. R.H.A.
R.O.,R.A. 5th.Cav. Divn.

Army Form C. 2118.

# WAR DIARY or INTELLIGENCE SUMMARY.
(Erase heading not required.)

17th Brigade R.H.A.

June 1917

| Place | Date | Hour | Summary of Events and Information | Remarks and references to Appendices |
|---|---|---|---|---|
| NOBESCOURT FARM. | From 1st | - | Batteries of 17th Bde. R.H.A. together with R.H.A. Bdes. forming the artillery of 5th Cav. Divn. are as arranged to A/253 Bingo Bty. | R.H.Hdqrs. |
| DIVNL. H.Q. | | | R.E.A. in action covering the cavalry holding the dismounted sector. 28th Hvy Artillery Group. forming the heavy artillery of the division. Sore wounded details was held by his Brigades to his line, and his hvy. | 1/43,000 trench 62 b 626 |
| " | 3rd | - | N Battery R.H.A. shelled heavily by hostile hvy battery – 100 rounds. Probably 15"cm. Being Known casualties 2 men slightly wounded. No damage to materiel. | 62 b 626 |
| " | 5th | - | Col. Roy. R.C.H.A. arrived on a 3 days visit to the R.C.H.A. Batteries | |
| " | 9/10 - | - | At. mid. night the enemy attempted to raid SOMERVILLE WOOD with 2 groups. 600 were driven off. Batteries fired 600 rounds in connection with this and night the enemy reported massing opposite RED WOOD. On guns | |
| " | 10th | - | Opened fire on a cer plane with artillery defence scheme, and the hostile concentration was broken up. No attack developed. Weather conditions changed, and at this time thunderstorms and of frequent occurrence causing much damage to telephone wires in exchanges. | |

| Place | Date | Hour | Summary of Events and Information | Remarks and references to Appendices |
|---|---|---|---|---|
| Reninghelst June | 12th | | Raid on ASCENSION WOOD carried out by Life Brigade supported by artillery fire from our batteries. Gas enemy sent into in the main trench, which was executed successfully, but a lot of enemy were met in the raiding party so caused a large battle, partial & unsuccessful, was counted. Our enemy was troubled. | |
| | 13th | | H.R.H. Bailiff joins the Brigade from England, and is posted to B Battery RHA. | |
| Vlamertinghe N? | | | U Battery RHA. fronts action under orders of 2d Cav. Div. to assist in a new advance. | |
| Poperinghe | 18th-19th | | Rifle Brigade carried out a very successful attack against the salient in the enemy's line near ST HELENE. 18 casualty officers & killed representing the total known, which then later his from Co. Brigade carries out extensive firing in conjunction with this. | |
| | 19th | | Lieut Dunraven - Brigade Orderly Officer to hospital with fever. No 39 C.C.S. | |
| | 23rd | | Lt Dunraven returns from hospital. | |
| | 25th | | Inspection by Staff | |

(E. Stephen)
by order h G.O.C.
f. R/Bt. N.of Gent of f. RHA. Bde
17.

W. Diary

## 5th. CAVALRY DIVISIONAL ARTILLERY OPERATION ORDER NO. 5.

Copy No. Spare

REFERENCE MAP
BELLENGLISE SHEET 2nd. EDITION.
1/20,000.                                                     June 1st, 1917.

1. The Artillery of the 5th. Cavalry Division will carry out wire-cutting and a bombardment of the enemy's trenches about ST. HELENE on the 2nd. June 1917 and during the night of the 2/3 June in accordance with the attached table, with the object of destroying his wire and trenches, killing his working parties and reinforcements and generally harassing him.

2. The 28th. Heavy Artillery Group will co-operate with a deliberate destructive shoot on the ST. HELENE trench between M.3.a.85.65 and M.3.a.9.9. to commence at 12 noon 2/5/17.

3. Ammunition to be expended must be dumped at the guns in excess of the dump already maintained.

4. Watches will be synchronized at 5th. Cavalry Divisional Artillery advanced Headquarters (R.8.b.central) at 12 noon on the 2nd. June.

5. Acknowledge by wire.

                                                    Lt. Col. R.C.H.A.
                                              For 5th. Cav.Divn.Artillery.

Copy No. 1.    Filed.
         2.    N. Battery. R.H.A.
         3.    X. Battery R.H.A.
         4.    A. Battery R.C.H.A.
         5.    B. Battery R.C.H.A.
         6.    A/295th. Bde. R.F.A.
         7.    D/298th. Bde.  "
         8.    28th. H.A.G.
         9.    R.H.A. Cav. Corps.
        10.    5th. Cavalry Divn.
        11.    Secunderabad Cav. Bde.
        12.    Canadian Cav. Bde.
        13 — 87th. French Division.
        14     5th Cav. Divn Arty
        14 - 22    Spare.

TABLE "A"

To accompany 5th.Cav.Divn.Arty.Operation Order No.5.

WIRE CUTTING

| Battery. | Wire to be cut. | Time. | No. of rounds allotted. | Total number of rounds. |
|---|---|---|---|---|
| A. Battery R.C.H.A. | M.3.c.7.7. – M.3.c.7.8. | Start when ordered after finish of H.A. Shoot (about 2.p.m.) | 40 Rounds per Gun N. | 160 N |
| B. Battery R.C.H.A. | M.3.c.7.8. – M.3.c.7.9. | Start on completion of A.Battery's Shoot. | 40 Rounds per gun. N. | 160. N. |
| N. Battery R.H.A. | G.33.d.05.8.– G.33.d.05.9. | Start when ordered after finish of B.A Shoot (about 2.p.m.) | 40 Rounds per gun N. | 240 N |
| K. Battery R.H.A. | G.33.d.05.9.– G.33.b.1.0. | Start on completion of N.Battery's Shoot. | 40 Rounds per gun N. | 240 N. |
| | | | Total | 800 N |

[signature]
Lt. Col. R.C.H.A.
For 5th.Cavalry Divisional Artillery.

# TABLE "B"
## To accompany 5th.Cav.Divn.Artillery Operation Order No.5.

| Battery. | 1st. Objective. | Time. | Rate of Fire. | 2nd. Objective. | Time. | Rate of Fire. | 3rd. Objective. | Time. | Rate of fire. | Total No. rounds. N. NX. BX. |
|---|---|---|---|---|---|---|---|---|---|---|
| A. R.C.H.A. | FISHER'S CRATER M.2.d.8.5. | 11.45.pm to 11.46.pm. 2/5/17. | 4 rds pr.gun pr.min. NX. | ST.HELENE TRENCH between M.3.d.4.65 and M.3.a.8.0. | 11.46.pm. to 11.50.pm. 2/5/17. | 2 rds. pr.gun per min. N.&NX. | Same as Second. | 2.30.a.m. to 2.35.am 3/5/17. | 2 rds pr.gun pr.min. NX | — 88 |
| B. R.C.H.A. | Sunken Road between M.3.a.I.8 and G.33.c.I.3. | 11.45.pm to 11.46.pm. 2/5/17. | 4 rds. pr.gun pr.min. N.X. | ST.HELENE TRENCH between M.3.a.8.0. and M.3.a.9.9. | 11.46.pm to 11.50.pm. 2/5/17. | 2 rds. pr.gun pr.min N.& NX. | ST.HELENE ROAD between M.3.b.5.0. and M.4.a.0.4. | 2.30.am to 2.35.am 3/5/17. | 2 rds pr.gun pr.min N.& NX. | 36 52 — |
| N. R.H.A. 4 guns. | Communication trench between M.3.a.9.9. and G.34.c.0.2. | 11.45.pm to | 2 rds. per gun per min. NX | Same as First Objective. | 2.30.am to 2.35.am 3/5/17 | 2 rds. per gun per min. N. NX | | | | |
| 2 guns. | ELEVEN TREES G.33.c.8.6. - G.33.a.6.I. | | | | | | | | | 60. 60. |
| X. R.H.A. | SQUARE COPSE G.35.b.0.6. and trench between G33d.0.2-G33b.I.6. | 11.45.pm to 11.50.pm. 2/5/17. | 2 rds. per gun pr.min. N.& NX. | Same as first Objective. | 2.30.am. to 2.35.am 3/5/17. | 2 rds. pr.gun pr.min N.& NX | | | | 60. 60. |
| ∆/295. | Trench, Sunken Rd. & bank between M.3.a.9.9. — G33d.0.2.-G.33c.8.6 G.33.d.I.9. | 11.45.pm to 11.50.pm 2/5/17. | 2 rds. pr.gun pr.min N. NX | Same as First Objective. | 2.30.am. to 2.35.am 3/5/17. | 2 rds. pr.gun pr.min N. NX. | | | | 60. |
| D/298. I Howr. | SQUARE COPSE G.35.b.0.6. | 11.45.pm to 11.50.pm. 2/5/17. | 2 rds. pr.How pr.min BX. | Dugouts and road about M.3.b.3.4. | 2.30.am. to 2.35.am 3/5/17. | 2 rds. pr.How per min BX | | | | 60. |
| 2 Howr. | Sunken road and bank between G33d.0.2-G33.c.8.6 G.33.d.I.9. | | | | | | | | | — — 6 |
| | | | | | | | | | Total Rds. | 216 320 60 |

Lt.Col.R.C.H.A.

# 5th. CAVALRY DIVISIONAL ARTILLERY OPERATION ORDER NO. 6

Copy No.

REFERENCE MAP. 1/20,000.
BELLENGLISE SHEET 2nd. EDITION

June 10th, 1917.

1. The Artillery of the Division will carry out a short bombardment of the Enemy's Trench System between INK ALLEY (M.3.a.9.9.) and WATLING STREET (G.27.d.0.5.) at 6.00.p.m. to day 10.6.17, in accordance with the attached table, with the object of retaliation.

2. The 28th. H.A.G. will co-operate.

3. Watches will be synchronized at Advanced Headquarters (R.8.b. central at 4.00.p.m. this date.

4. Acknowledge.

---

## Bombardment Table.

| Battery. | Objective. | Time. | Rate of fire. | No. of rounds. | | | | |
|---|---|---|---|---|---|---|---|---|
| | | | | N. | NX. | A | AX. | BX. |
| N. RHA. | Trench System G.33.d.9.9. - G.33.b.1.6. | 6.00.p.m. to 6.04.p.m. 6.03 pm | 4 rounds per gun per min. | 48. 36 | 48. 36 | | | |
| X. RHA. | Trench system G.33.b.1.6. - G.27.d.1.3. | do. | do. | 48. 36 | 48. 36 | | | |
| A. RCHA | Sunken road G.33.d.0.2. - G.33.c.8.6. | do. | do. | 32. 24 | 32. 24 | | | |
| B. RCHA. | ELEVEN TREES & Bank G.33.c.8.6. - G.33.d.1.85. | do. | do. | 32. 24 | 32. 24 | | | |
| A/295. | Trench System about WATLING STREET G.27.d.1.2. - G.27.Central. | do. | do. | | | 48. 36 | 48. 36 | |
| D/298. | New Trench between G.33.d.5.0. and G.33.d.1.8. | do. | 2 Rounds per gun per minute. | 120 | 120 | 36 | 36 | 18 24 18 |
| | | | Total | 160 | 160 | 48. | 48. | 24. |

Lt. Col. R.C.H.A.
For 5th. Cav. Divn. Artillery.

Copy No. 1. Filed.
2. N. R.H.A.
3. X. R.H.A.
4. A. R.C.H.A.
5. B. R.C.H.A.
6. A/295.
7. D/298.
8. Cavalry Corps.
9. 5th.Cav.Division.
10. Ambala Cav. Bde
11. Secunderabad Cav. Bde.

Secret

5th CAVALRY DIVISIONAL ARTILLERY O.O. NO. 7
------------------------------------------------

Copy No. 15

Reference Map 1/20,000
BELLENGLISE SHEET 2nd. Edition.

June 12th, 1917.

1. The SECUNDERABAD CAVALRY BRIGADE will raid ASCENSION WOOD to-night at zero hour with one Squadron.
   They will enter the Wood from the West and S.W. side, and patrols will be pushed forward to search the whole wood. Zero hour will be notified later.

2. In accordance with the above, the 5th. Cav.D.A. together with two Batteries of the 4th.Cav.D.A. will form a barrage as shown in attached table.

3. Corps Heavy Artillery will co-operate by bombarding BIG BILL and trench system between WATLING STREET and BUISSON-GAULAINE FM including the latter.

4. Ammunition will be dumped at the guns for this operation in excess of that already there.

5. Watches will be synchronized at advanced Artillery H.Q. (R.8.b) at 7.00 p.m. to-day - a representative being sent from each Battery for this purpose.

6. Acknowledge by wire.

Lt. Col. R.C.H.A.
For 5th. Cavalry Divn. Artillery.

Copy No. 1 - 3   4th.Cav.D.A.
       4.    N. R.H.A.
       5.    X. R.H.A.
       6.    A / 295.
       7.    D / 298.
       8.    R.H.A. Cav.Corps.
       9.    G. 5th.Cav. Divn.
      10.    Secunderabad Cav.Bde.
      11.    Ambala Cav. Bde.
      12.    A.D.M.S.
      13.    A. R.C.H.A. ) For information.
      14.    B. R.C.H.A. )
      15 - 18. War Diary.

# 5th. CAVALRY DIVISIONAL ARTILLERY

Barrage Table to accompany Operation Order No.7.

| Battery. | 1st. Objective. | Time. | Rate of Fire | 2nd. Objective. | Time. | Rate of Fire. | Total No of Rounds. | | | | |
|---|---|---|---|---|---|---|---|---|---|---|---|
| | | | | | | | N. | NX. | A. | A&NX | BX. |
| B/ 295. | G.19.d.5.5.– LITTLE BILL (inclusive) | Zero to zero+30' | 2 rounds per gun per min. A. AX. | ---- | --- | --- | | | 120 | 120. | |
| "Q" R.H.A. | LITTLE BILL (exclusive) – G.26.a.6@.75. | Zero to zero +30' | 2 rounds per gun per min N. NX. | --- | --- | --- | 180. | 180. | | | |
| A / 295. | G.25.a.60.75.– G.26.a.6.0. | Zero to zero +30' | 2 rounds per gun per min A. AX | --- | --- | --- | | | 180. | 180. | |
| "X" R.H.A. | G.26.a.6.0.– G.26.c.0.5. | Zero to zero +30' | 2 rounds per gun per min N.NX. | --- | --- | --- | 180. | 180. | | | |
| "N" R.H.A. | G.25.d.6.4.– G.26.c/3.6. | do. | do. | --- | --- | --- | 180. | 180. | | | |
| D / 298. | ASCENSION WOOD working from West to East. | Zero to zero +3' | 2 rounds per gun per min BX. | 1 Howr. LITTLE BILL 2 Howr. BIG BILL | zero +3½ zero +30' | 1 rd per gun per min BX. | | | | | 99 |
| | | | | | | Total rounds 540. | 540. | 540. | 300. | 300. | 99 |

Total rounds 540.

M.H.P. Slo........
for .... Cav. ........

SECRET
Headquarters,
5th. Cav.Divn.Arty.

S/78/G
June 12th, 1917.

To:- 4th. Cavalry Div.Arty.
N. Battery R.H.A.
X.   "        "
A.   "     295th.Bde.R.F.A.
D.   "     298th.Bde. R.F.A.
G.S. 5th.Cav. Divn.

---

Reference 5th. Cavalry Divisional Artillery Operation Order No.7. of this date, para 1.

The raiding party will enter ASCENSION WOOD from the North, starting from the Line G.25.b.8.9. - G.26.a.0.8. - G.26.a.2.7. instead of as therein stated.

Lt. Col. R.C.H.A.
For 5th. Cav. Div'l Artillery.

Copy to:-
A. R.C.H.A.
B. R.C.H.A.

---

SECRET

S/78/G

Headquarters,
5th. Cav. Divn.Arty.

June 12th, 1917.

To:- 4th.Cav.Divn.Arty.
N. Battery R.H.A.
X. Battery R.H.A.
A.   "     295th.Bde.R.F.A.
D.   "     298th.Bde.R.F.A.

---

Reference 5th.Cav.Divn.Artillery O.O. No. 7

Zero Hour is 2.00.a.m. 13.6.17.

Lt. Col. R.C.H.A.
For 5th. Cav. Divn.Artillery.

---

SECRET.
H.Q., 5th.Cav. D.A.

June 12th, 1917.

To:- 4th.Cav.Div.Arty.
N. Battery R.H.A.
X.   "        "
A.   "     295th.Bde.R.F.A.
D.   "     298th.Bde.R.F.A.

---

Reference Table of Barrages issued with 5th.Cav Div.Arty.O.O.No.7.,

The 1st.Objective of D/298 will be the Southern Edge of ASCENSION WOOD only, and not as therein stated, and will last from zero to zero 2 minutes only when they will lift to 2nd. Objective.

The 1st.Objective of N.Bty R.H.A. will be G.28.a.0.5 - G.26.a.6.0. and not as stated in the above table.

Lt. Col. R.C.H.A.
For 5th. Cavalry.Divn.Arty.

Copy to:-
A. R.C.H.A.
B. R.C.H.A.

SECRET.

## 5th. CAVALRY DIVISIONAL ARTILLERY OPERATION ORDER NO. 8

Reference Map 1/20,000             Copy No......
BELLENGLISE SHEET 2nd.Edition.

June 14th, 1917.

1. With the intention of harassing the enemy, the undermentioned Batteries of the Divisional Artillery will fire on BIG BILL to-day 14-6-17 for 2 minutes commencing at 3.00.p.m.
    Rate of fire:-
        4 Rounds per gun per minute 13 and 18 pounders.
        2 Rounds per How.per minute 4.5 Howrs.

    N. Battery R.H.A.
    X. Battery R.H.A.
    A. Battery 295th.Bde. R.F.A.
    D. Battery 298th.Bde. R.F.A.

2. 50% Shrapnel and 50% H.E. to be used by 13 and 18 pr. Batteries.

3. Watches will be synchronized at 2.00.p.m. by telephone from these Headquarters. An Officer of each Battery will be at the telephone for this purpose.

4. Acknowledge by wire.

                         Lt. Col. R.C.H.A.
                  For 5th.Cavalry Divn.Artillery.

Copy No. 1. N.Battery R.H.A.
        2. X.   "     "
        3. A.   "   295th.Bde.R.F.A.
        4. D.   "   298th.Bde.R.F.A.
        5. A.   "   R.C.H.A.
        6. B.   "     "
        7. R.H.A. Cavalry Corps.
        8. 5th.Cavalry Divn.
        9. Secunderabad Cav.Bde.
      10. Ambala Cav.Bde.
      11. A.D.M.S.
      12 to 15- War Diary

SECRET.

## 5th. CAVALRY DIVISIONAL ARTILLERY O.O. No.9

Reference Map 1/20,000           Copy No......17....
BELLENGLISE Sheet 2nd.Edition        June 16th, 1917.

1.     At Zero hour, on the night 18th/19th June 1917, a raid will be carried out against the enemy's front line trench and roads in the vicinity of ST.HELENE, with the object of cleaning out that Sector, and securing identifications.

2.     Zero hour will be signalled by the explosion of two Bangalore Torpedoes in M.3.a.8.6, the firing of a red and a green Very Light at the same point, and by the appearance of a rocket at the TUMULUS.

3.     The Artillery of the Division will assist the above operations by barrage fire in accordance with the attached table, and in order to create a diversion from Zero to Zero 45' two Batteries of the 4th.Cavalry Division ( if not required by their own Division) will place barrages on the following points :-

       G.20.c.4.7. - G.20.d.0.2.
       G.20.a.7.2. - G.20.d.5.4.

Two 6" Howitzers at the same time firing on BUISSON - GAULAINE FME and trenches S.E. of it.

4.     The Cavalry Corps Heavy Artillery will co-operate as follows:-

    (a) Four 6" Hows. on trench from G.33.d.5.0. - G.33.d.1.0.
        Four 6" Hows. from ELEVEN TREES to point where road crosses trench G.33.d.0.2. paying particular attention to the latter.
        Two 6" Hows. on SQUARE COPSE and the strong posts in G.33.b.4.3.

        Rate of fire one round per How. per minute from zero to zero+ 10.
        One round per How, per 2 minutes zero+ 10 to zero+ 45.

    (b) Four 60 pounders on the area bounded by M.4.b.7.0 - M.4.d.7.5. - M.5.c.5.5. - M.5.a.5.0.

        Four 60 pounders on the area G.33.d.5.4. - G.34.d.0.4. - G.34.b.0.0. - G.33.b.5.0. Bursts of fire at uncertain intervals from zero+10' to zero+55'. 15 Rounds per gun.

5.     The French Artillery, three Batteries of 75's, have been asked to barrage from
       G.33.d.5.0. - M.4.c.5.5.

One Battery 155's from G.34.c.0.2. - G.34.c.5.3. - M.4.a.6.8. - M.4.b.0.7.

One Battery 105's on the Bridge and approaches in G.34.d.central.

6.     Ammunition for this enterprise must be dumped at the guns in excess of that already kept with them.

7.     Acknowledge by wire

                                       Lt. Col. R.C.H.A.
                                       For 5th.Cav.Divn.Arty.

Copy No.1. N.Battery.R.H.A.
       2. U.Battery. "
       3. K.Battery. "
       4. A.Battery R.C.H.A.     11. 5th.Cav.Divn.
       5. B.   "                  12. Cav.Corps H.A.
       6. / 295.               13. French Artillery.
       7. / 293               14. " "
       8. R.H.A.Cav.Corps.      15. A.D.M.S.
       9. Ambala Cav.Bde.       16 to 20. War Diary.
      10. Canadian Cav.Bde.

# 5th. CAVALRY DIVISIONAL ARTILLERY.

### Barrage Table to accompany Operation Order No. 8.

| Battery. | 1st. Objective. | Time. | Rate of fire. | 2nd. Objective. | Time. | Rate of fire. | Number of rounds. N. | NX. | A. | AX. | B. | BX. |
|---|---|---|---|---|---|---|---|---|---|---|---|---|
| A. R.C.H.A. | Road at M.3.c.8.6. | Zero to zero+5' | 4 rds. per gun per min N. NX. | ST.HELENE-BELLENGLISE road M.4.a.0.4.- M.4.a.70.75. | Zero+5' to zero +45' | 2 rds. per gun per min N. NX. | | | | | | |
| M. R.H.A. | INK ALLEY G.33.d.5.0.- M.3.a.95.90. | Zero to zero +45' | 2 rds. per gun per min N. NX. | | | | 200. | 200. | | | | |
| B'. R.C.H.A. | INK ALLEY G.33.d.5.0.- G.34.c.0.2. | Zero to zero +45' | do. | | | | 270. | 270. | | | | |
| D. 298. | INK ALLEY G.34.c.0.2.- G.33.d.5.0. | Zero to zero +15' | 1 rd. per How. per min. BX. | INK ALLEY G.33.d.5.0.- M.3.b.2.7. | Zero+15' to zero +45' | 1 rd per How. per min BX. | 180. | 180. | | | | 135. |
| U. R.H.A. 2 sections | Trench between G.33.d.0.2.-M.3.a.95.90. | Zero to zero +45' | 2 rds. per gun per min N. NX. | | | | | | | | | |
| 1 section | On area enclosed by G.33.d.5.5.-G.33.d.5.3.- G.33.d.8.3.-G.33.d.8.5. | | | | | | 270. | 270. | | | | |
| X. R.H.A. | Sunken road and Bank - G.33.d.0.2.-G.33.c.8.6. G.33.d.1.9. | Zero to zero +45' | do. | | | | 270. | 270. | | | | |
| A. 298. | SQUARE COPSE and trench G.33.b.2.6. G.33.d.1.9. | Zero to zero +45' | 2 rds per gun per min. A. AX | | | | | | 270. | 270. | | |
| | | | | | | Total rounds. | 1190. | 1190. | 270. | 270. | 135. | 135. |

*W.H.P. Stephens* Lt. Col. R.C.H.A.
For 5th. Cavalry Divisional Artillery.

SECRET

## 5th. CAVALRY DIVISIONAL ARTILLERY O. O. No. 10.

Reference Map 1/20,000
BELLENGLISE SHEET 2nd.EDITION

Copy No. 16

June 21st, 1917.

1. Information has been received that a hostile relief is due on the night of the 21.6.17 in the BELLENGLISE Sector.
Prisoners state that the usual routine is for the relief to arrive at LA BARAQUE about 10.30.p.m., halt there until 10.45.p.m., and then move on.

2. Two short heavy bursts of fire are therefore being arranged for on the road from BELLENGLISE to about G.30.c.0.9. The Heavy Artillery co-operating with the 5th.Cavalry Divisional Artillery.

3. In accordance with the above:- N. Battery R.H.A., B. Bty R.C.H.A. and D.Battery 298th.Bde.R.F.A. will fire on the under-mentioned Objectives from 10.33. to 10.36.p.m. and from 10.41 to 10. 44.p.m. to-day .
Rate of fire 6 rounds per gun per minute: 2 rounds per Howr. per minute. :-

Advanced gun "N" R.H.A. on LA BARAQUE cross roads.

D/298 on LA BARAQUE cross roads.

"B" R.C.H.A. on road from G.35.a.2.2. to LA BARAQUE cross roads.

Five guns "N" R.H.A. on road G.35.a.2.2. to LA BARAQUE.

4. Any necessary registration to be carried out well clear of the road.

5. The BERTHAUCOURT O.P. is now connected by a 28th.H.A.G. wire to the O.P. exchange, and is available for use this afternoon.

6. Acknowledge by wire.

Lt. Col. R.C.H.A.
For 5th.Cav. Divn. Artillery.

Copy No.1. N. R.H.A.
    2. X. R.H.A.
    3. A. R.C.H.A.
    4  B. R.C.H.A.
    5. A/295.
    6. D/298.
    7. Cav.Corps R.H.A.
    8. 28th. H.A.G.
    9. Ambala Cav.Bde.
  10. Canadian Cav.Bde.
  11. Cav. Corps H. A.
  12. 5th. Cav.Division.
  13. French Artillery.
  14. A.D.M.S.
  15. to 18.War Diary.

SECRET

## 5th. CAVALRY DIVISIONAL ARTILLERY O.O. No.11.

Ref. Map 1/20,000.
LELLENGLISE SHEET 2nd. Edition.

Copy No.

22. 6. 17.

1. With the object of destroying the trenches, and distracting the enemy's attention from a proposed raid, day and night firing will be carried out on INK ALLEY and the NEW TRENCH in G.33.d., being taken up from receipt of this order.

2. The following batteries will take part, firing on the objectives shown :-

    "N" R.H.A. on NEW TRENCH between G.33.d.5.0 - G.33.d.35.50.

    "X" R.H.A. on NEW TRENCH between G.33.d.35.50 - G.33.d.1.9.

    "_" R.C.H.A. on INK ALLEY between G.33.d.5.0. - G.34.c.0.2.

    "D" R.C.H.A. on INK ALLEY between G.34.c.0.2. - G.34.c.5.3.

3. Times of firing will be as follows :-

    "N" R.H.A.   10.00.a.m. to 12.noon.
                   6.00.p.m. to 8.00.p.m.
                   2.00.a.m. to 4.00.a.m.

    "X" R.H.A.   12.noon to 2.00.p.m.
                   8.00.p.m. to 10.00.p.m.
                 4.00.a.m. to 6.00.a.m.

    "_" R.C.H.A.  6.00.a.m. to 8.00.a.m.
                    2.00.p.m. to 4.00.p.m.
                  10.00.p.m. to 12 midnight.

    "D" R.C.H.A.  8.00.a.m. to 10.00.a.m.
                    4.00.p.m. to 6.00.p.m.
                  12 midnight to 2.00.a.m.

4. Each battery will fire 20 rounds H.E. during each period of two hours allotted to it. Times of firing and rate of fire should be made as irregular as the two hours allow.

5. H.E. being allotted for this task, shrapnel must be used on other targets in order to keep to the daily expenditure of 50, H.E. and 50 Shrapnel.

6. This bombardment will continue until further orders.

7. Acknowledge.

                                       J.W. Hughes Capt.
                                       for Lt. Col. R.C.H.A.
                                       For 5th. Cav. Divn. Artillery.

Copy No. 1. to N. R.H.A.
     2. " X. R.H.A.
     3. " A. R.C.H.A.
     4. " L. R.C.H.A.
     5. " ./295.
     6. " D/293.
     7. " M.E.F. Cav. Corps.
     8. " 5th. Cav. Divn.
     9. " 28th. H.A.G.
    10. French Artillery.
    11. Canadian Cav. Bde.
    12. Ambala Cav. Bde.
    13 to 16 War Diary.
    17 Secunderabad Cav Bde

S E C R E T

## 5TH. CAVALRY DIVISIONAL ARTILLERY O.O. No. 12.

Ref.Map 1/20,000                          Copy No.....
BELLENGLISE Sheet 2nd.Edition

26.6.17.

     The bombardment ordered in 5th. Cavalry Divn'l Artillery Operation Order No.11 will cease for 24 hours at 8.00.p.m. to-day.

     It will re-open at 8.00.p.m. the 27th instant.

                                            Lt.Col.R.C.H.A.
                                For 5th.Cav.Divn.Artillery.

Copy No. 1.     N. R.H.A.
        2.     X.  "
        3.     A. R.C.H.A.
        4      E.  "
        5      A/ 295.
        6.     D/ 298.
        7.     R.H.A. Cav.Corps
        8.     5th. Cav.Divn.
        9.     28th.H.A.G.
       11.     Canadian Cav.Bde.
       12.     Ambala Cav.Bde.
       13.     Secunderabad Cav.Bde.
       14.     French Artillery.

SECRET

COPY NO. ___

5th. CAVALRY DIVISIONAL ARTILLERY INSTRUCTIONS No. 1

June 25th, 1917

1. Patrols of R.C.Ds. and L.S.H. will reconnoitre the Quarry in G.20.d.central to-night, leaving our lines at 11.00.p.m.

2. In the eventuality of heavy rifle and machine gun fire being opened on them from the enemy trenches in G.20 and 21, the following batteries will be prepared to open fire :-

    A / 295 on trenches G.20.a.9.6. - G.20.b.6.1.

    N. R.H.A. on trenches G.20.b.6.1. - G.21.c.0.5.

    X. R.H.A. on trenches G.21.c.0.5. - G.21.c.5.0.

Rate of fire one round per gun per minute.

3. F.O.O. A / 295 will be responsible for opening and ceasing fire.

H.Q. 5th.Cav.D.A.

Lt. Col. R.C.H.A.
For 5th. Cavalry Divn. Artillery

Copy No. 1 N. Battery R.H.A.
    2. X. Battery R.H.A.
    3. A.  "   295th. Bde. R.F.A.
    4. A.  "   R.C.H.A.
    5. B.  "   "
    6. D.  "   298th. Bde. R.F.A.
    7. Canadian Cav. Bde.
    8. Secunderabad Cav. Bde.
    9. 5th. Cavalry Division.

SECRET                                                    Copy No.......

## 5th. CAVALRY DIVISIONAL ARTILLERY INSTRUCTIONS No. 2

June 26th, 1917

1. In consequence of our withdrawal from SOMERVILLE WOOD. new S.O.S. barrages have been arranged for as shown in this office No.S/50/3/G.
   These barrages will not be registered by X. R.H.A., A. and E R.C.H.A., as their registration would give information to the enemy Those Batteries will however, by registration to the front of these lines etc., ensure the greatest possible accuracy should shooting on these lines be required.
   A sketch showing the zones of S.O.S. Lines has been issued to all concerned.

2. The above changes have also altered the Mutual Support Schemes, and a new Table of Mutual Support Schemes - No.S/52/4/G - has been issued. This does away with "Defend SOMERVILLE WOOD" and replaces it by "Defend LONE TREE"

3. The attached sketches and the following explanation, it is hoped, will lead to a more thorough comprehension as to how Artillery support can be most rapidly obtained at any point, and exactly what effect the code calls will have

   (a) The effect of the code call "Defend ASCENSION FARM" is to bring down S.O.S. barrages from "N" R.H.A. and A/295. These barrages being thickened by "X" R.H.A..
   Other Batteries do not fire.

   (b) The effect of the call "Defend RED WOOD" is to bring down S.O.S. barrages from "N" and "X" R.H.A. thickened by "B" RCHA
   Other Batteries do not fire.

   (c) The effect of the code call "Defend LONE TREE" is to bring down S.O.S. barrages from "X" R.H.A. and "B" RCHA Thickened by
   Other Batteries do not fire.                          "N" R.H.A.

4. The quickest way to obtain any of these local barrages is to telephone direct to C.H.S. and simply give the code call, and the Office of origin, to the telephonist. It is not necessary to obtain an Officer.

5. It should be borne in mind that these barrages are put down <u>close</u> in front of our outpost Line, so would catch any of our wiring parties or patrols who might be out in front of that Sector

                                              [signature]
                                              Lt. Col. R.C.H.A.
                                         For 5th.Cav.Div. Artillery.

Copy No.1. 5th.Cav.Div.
       2. N. R.H.A.
       3. X. R.H.A.
       4. A. R.C.H.A.
       5. B. R.C.H.A.
       6. A/ 295.
       7. D/ 298.
       8. Cavalry Corps.
       9. Canadian Cav.Bde.
      10. Secunderabad Cav.Bde.
      11. Ambala Cav. Bde.
      12. French Artillery.

S E C R E T.  Copy No. ....

## 5th. CAVALRY DIVISIONAL ARTILLERY INSTRUCTIONS No. 3.

June 29th, 1917.

1. A raid on COLOGNE FARM is to be carried out by the 4th. Cavalry Division at Zero-hour on "Z" day.

A/295 and D/298 Batteries 5th. Cavalry Divisional Artillery will co-operate in accordance with the attached schelude and map.

2. Zero hour will be communicated later.

3. Registration will take place to-day, and there will be no further firing on these points until "Z" day.

4. Should a S.O.S. go up on 5th. Cavalry Divisional front during operations, one section of A/295 and one Howitzer D/298 will continue to take part in this operation - remainder turning on to S.O.S. Lines.

5. Ammunition is authorized in excess of daily allotment.

6. Acknowledge by wire.

Lt.Col.R.C.H.A.
For 5th.Cav.Divn.Artillery.

Copy No. 1. A/295.
       2. D/298.
       3. & 4 Filed.

Army Form C. 2118.

# WAR DIARY
or
# INTELLIGENCE SUMMARY.

(Erase heading not required.)

July. Heads Quarters News & Batteries 17th Bde. R.F.A.

| Place | Date | Hour | Summary of Events and Information | Remarks and references to Appendices |
|---|---|---|---|---|
| NOBESCOURT FARM. | 1st. | — | N and X batteries fired a Chinese barrage in support of a raid on CROISILLE FARM by the division on our left. | Raid unsuccessful. Ref Rapho S.1/400. 62c & 62b. |
| " | 3rd. | — | Col. W.G. Thompson Cmdg. 152nd Bde. R.F.A. 34th Divn Artillery, arrived to discuss details of reliefs. | |
| " | 6th. | — | BACK AREAS near CAULAINCOURT shelled by enemy long range gun doing considerable damage. In return for this we bombarded the villages of BELLENGLISE - LA BERGÈRE - LA BARAQUE - LEHAUCOURT - ESTRÉES and ÉTRICOURT with all batteries including 6" hows & 60 pdrs. | |
| " | 6th-7th | — | Raid on vicinity of the "SEVEN TREES" B.3.g.7.d.5.5.5. 4 enemy lay wounded, and identifications obtained, no prisoners. Batteries put down a box barrage round the area raided. | |
| " | 7th | — | 2Lt. J.B. SMITH, and 2Lt. J.A.M. BOND joined the brigade from the base in attached to N and X horse artillery. | |
| " | — | — | Raid on the enemy trench system to the south of SOISSON GAILLAINE FARM, carried out by Canadian Cav. Bde. All batteries fired in connection with this raid, and support was also given by batteries of 4th Cav Div. on our left, and by the French on our right. The raid was very successful. 10 M.Gs & 35 prisoners & a machine gun being taken. | |

2353  Wt. W2544/1454  700,000  5/15  D. D. & L.    A.D.S.S./Forms/C. 2118.

Army Form C. 2118.

# WAR DIARY or INTELLIGENCE SUMMARY.
(Erase heading not required.)

| Place | Date | Hour | Summary of Events and Information | Remarks and references to Appendices |
|---|---|---|---|---|
| NOREUIL FARM. | 8th | 9 pm | Two fine pairs in the raided area were reported active, and it was hoped that these guns met a runner officer and 2 teams & a party of 40 R.E's, accompanied the raiding party for this purpose. The pits were found, but were unoccupied, and unfortunately the Officer — Lieut. J. Stewart R.G.H.A. — was killed by a shell burst while on the way back. A great many casualties were inflicted on the enemy, while no one was slight. All ranks of the raiding party appeared contented by the excellence of the barrage. | |
| " | 9th | | A. Battery R.G.H.A. On the southern flank near VENDENCOURT CHATEAU were heavily shelled by a S.F. battery firing from MACNY 10.F28E and a 4.2 battery firing from near NAUROY. The four carriages were considerably shifted about, and spokes splintered etc. but pieces were not damaged. — No casualties. The French being artillery assisted in by neutralising the S.F. battery, later they carried out a destructive shoot in this battery and a large explosion was caused. Col. W.G. Thompson & relieving battery Commanders visited battery positions. Relief of McCausley by infantry of 34th Divn. Completed. | |
| " | 10th | | X Battery heavily shelled by a 4.2 battery near NAUROY over 2 rounds. In spite of the efforts of our counter battery firing the hostile fire was very persistent. No damage done, no casualties. | |

Army Form C. 2118.

# WAR DIARY
## or
## INTELLIGENCE SUMMARY.
*(Erase heading not required.)*

Instructions regarding War Diaries and Intelligence Summaries are contained in F.S. Regs., Part II. and the Staff Manual respectively. Title pages will be prepared in manuscript.

| Place | Date | Hour | Summary of Events and Information | Remarks and references to Appendices |
|---|---|---|---|---|
| MORBECOURT FARM. | 10th | | 1 Section of each Battery relieved by a section of incoming Batteries. | Ref maps St QUENTIN AMIENS LENS 1/100,000 |
| " | 11th | | D/256 RFA. Withdraws to new position. | |
| | | | Artillery relief completed, and command handed over to Brig. Genl. Wallah also R.A. | |
| | | | Cmdg. Dft. 3rd Cav. Division. Head Qrs. 3rd Cav. R.H.A. report with rest of 3rd Cav. Div. HQ | |
| BOUVINCOURT | 12th | | at BOUVINCOURT. Batteries withdraw to new lines. | |
| | 13th 15th | | to new lines. | |
| | | | Cavalry move north. | |
| CAPPY. | 15th | | R.H.A. Batteries marching independently after last convoy bivaced at CAPPY for the night. 18 miles. Move off next day at 6.0 a.m. | |
| HEILLY. | 16th | | Marched from CAPPY to HEILLY, and HQ. billeted in HEILLY & to bivack. Batteries in MERICOURT. - 15 miles | |
| MERICOURT. ORVILLE AMPLIER AUTHUILLE | } 17th | | Marches from HEILLY to ORVILLE and vicinity. 20 miles. | |
| DOULLENS | | | | |
| St POL. | 18th | | Marched from ORVILLE area to St POL area. Head Qr. & Pos. Batteries to Brigade areas in neighbourhood of corps under orders of Cavalry Brigades. Bde. Cmdr. Lt. Col. Leveling sec. Dir. proceed on 10 days leave to PARIS. | diphtheria |

2333  Wt. W2544/1454  700,000  5/15  D.D. & L.  A.D.S.S./Forms/C. 2118.

Army Form C. 2118.

# WAR DIARY
## or
## INTELLIGENCE SUMMARY.
(Erase heading not required.)

Instructions regarding War Diaries and Intelligence Summaries are contained in F. S. Regs., Part II. and the Staff Manual respectively. Title pages will be prepared in manuscript.

| Place | Date | Hour | Summary of Events and Information | Remarks and references to Appendices |
|---|---|---|---|---|
| In Pos. | 15th | | N Bty | |
| — do — | 26th | | Major E.M. PROCTOR SMITH returns from leave to England. | LENS |
| — do — | 27th | 1.30am | In trenches. 2nd Lieut. BOYD proceeds to hosp. as orderly officer. Having telephone orders Rt. Sect. Batteries to Send up barrages in support to No. 1 Corps for attachment Canadian Corps. Experienced considerable shelling. Experienced Batt. Brigade at 5.0am. Brigade barrage attack 10.0pm no orders attached. Brig orders fired for him until, in the area GAVRELLE SENSE — OPPY — FRESNOY CT. Harassing continued 10.0 a.m. to noon. Lines — R.M.A. Batteries attached to 2nd CANADIAN DIVNL ARTILLERY — 153 R.A. Col PANET — under Grps 3th Divn M.A. | 1.100 am |
| BOUVIGNY LEGAL | 28th | | | |
| GRENAY SAIX | 29th | | NOULETTE & PULLY GRENAY. Batteries go into action in support of MAZINGARBE. Reps. being of situation this sector. Repts. being received but employed fatigues into motor lorries. R.O.T. missing. Bn. No Cas. Lt. Employed fatigues into motor lorries. R.O.T. missing. Return from leave, attached CANADIAN CORPS ARTILLERY H.Q. Bn. Artillery casualties CAPT & 1 White 2 W. Personnel, 1 OR Killed & 2 OR Wounded. | |
| — do — | 30th | | CAPT. E. ANDERSON Takes over temporary command of X Battery Btn. in interim Rept. WHITE during the absence return of Major Hon. WALKER D.S.O. | |
| — do — | 31st | | In action. | |

C.C. Smyth R.F.A.
Lt. Col. Comdg.
17 Bde R.F.A.

RHA
HQ

G.O.C. R.A.
Cavalry Corps. 29.6.17.

To/ C.R.H.A.
5th. Cav Div.

   The M.G. R.A. Fourth Army wishes me to convey his appreciation of the excellent work done by all ranks of the Artillery of the Cavalry Corps during their period in the Line under the Fourth Army.

         Signed H.S. Seligman. Brig Gen.
     G.O.C. R.A. Cavalry Corps.

G.39.

Headquarters,
5th.Cav.Divn.Arty.
July 9th, 1917.

To:- 17th Bde R.H.A.

Copy of a letter received by C.R.H.A. 9.7.17 from Col.
Paterson Commanding Canadian Cavalry Brigade.

Dear Colonel;

I wish you would thank for me the Batteries who did such fine work for us last night.

All reports agree that the barrages fell in the exact place where they were expected, and it may be of interest to you to know that our men worked under them with the greatest of confidence.

I very much appreciate the hard work done by the various Battery Commanders, and the care taken by them in registering in order to obtain these results.

I came into personal touch with Captain WASON of the 4.5's and Major WALKER of X.Battery, and I am sure that the success of the raid was largely due to the preliminary work done by those two Officers.

The Officer in charge of the advanced party tells me that he would have had great difficulty in locating the place for the torpedo had it not been for the periodical shells dropped by the 4.5's on the junction of A. and B. trenches.

I wish also to thank you for the way you stood behind us. From what I hear, the heavy expenditure of ammunition was fully justified by the number of the enemy who must have been killed by the barrage.

Sincerely,

R.R.Paterson.

SECRET

## 5th. CAVALRY DIVISIONAL ARTILLERY OPERATION ORDER No. 16

Ref. Corps Topo Section
No.14 1/10,000 Map d/18.6.17

Copy No......

July 7th. 1917

1. A raid will be carried out by Canadian Cavalry Brigade on the night of July 8th/9th against the enemy's trench line from G.21.c.5.0. to G.20.d.8.8. and the strong points in G.21.c.

2. Zero hour, approximately 11.30.p.m. will be indicated by the firing of a Bangalore Torpedo in the German wire at G.21.c.4.0.
    Green and Red Very lights will also be fired by the leader of the raiding party, and a Green and Red rocket from No.4.Post.

3. (a) The raiding party will leave the enemy's trenches at zero 45'

   (b) At zero+40' a green rocket will be fired from No.4.Post to warn the raiding party to withdraw.

4. The 5th.Cavalry Divisional Artillery will assist with the Bombardment and barrages as laid down in the attached table.

5. The 111.Corps Heavy Artillery will co-operate as follows :-

   6" Howitzers
   Zero to Zero+4', four Hows. on Trench G.21.c.20.85 to G.21.c.25.60. Two Hows. on Bank at G.21.c.30.75. Rate of fire 1 round per How. per minute.

   Zero+4' to zero+45', four Hows. on BUISSON GAULAINE FARM and Sunken Road and trench system         South to G.20.b.
   Two Hows. on trench junction at G.27.a.85.55.
   Rate of fire - 1 Round per How. per 2 minutes.

   60 Pounders.
   Zero to zero+5', two guns on trench system and Sunken Road from BUISSON GAULAINE FARM to G.20.b.3.0.
   One gun each on two tracks leading East from bank at G.21.c.30.75.
   Rate of fire 2 rds. per gun per minute. Shrapnel.

   Zero+5' to zero+45', two guns each on two tracks leading East from bank at G.21.c.30.75.
   Irregular bursts of fire, Shrapnel.

6. The French Artillery from Zero to zero+45' will fire on EWAN REDOUBT and WAT TRENCH as far North as G.27.central, with three Batteries, firing two rounds per gun per minute. Total 1100 rds.

7. Watches will be synchronized by telephone at 9.30.p.m. 8th inst. An Officer to be on the telephone at that time.

8. Acknowledge by wire.

Lt.Col.R.C.H.A
For 5th.Cav.Divn.Artillery

Copy No.1. N. Battery R.H.A.
    2. X.   "      "
    3. A.   "    R.C.H.A.
    4. B.   "      "
    5. A. / 295.
    6. D. / 298.
    7. 4th.Cav.Divn.Arty.
    8. 111. Corps H.A.
    9. 5th.Cav.Divn.
    10. R.H.A.Cav.Corps.
    12. Canadian Cav.Bde.
    13. Secunderabad Cav.Bde.
    14. French Artillery.
    15. A.D.M.S.
    16 to 18 War Diary.

Ref. 1/10,000 Map  Table of barrages to accompany 5th.Cavalry Div'l Artillery O.O.No.13
Corps Topo Section No.14.d/16.6.17

| Battery | 1st.Objective | Time | Rate of Fire | 2nd.Objective | Time | Rate of Fire | 3rd.Objective | Time | Rate of Fire | 4th.Objective | Time | Rate of Fire |
|---|---|---|---|---|---|---|---|---|---|---|---|---|
| B. R.C.H.A. | G.27.a.85.55. TO G.27.a.7.7. | Zero to zero +2' | 6 rds. per gun per min. | G.27.a.85.55. to G.27.b.0.8. | Zero +2' to zero +45' | ⊗ | G.27.a.85.55 to G.27.b.0.2. | Zero +45' to zero +60' | | | | |
| N. R.H.A. | G.27.a.7.7.to G.27.a.5.9. | do. | do. | G.27.b.0.8. to G.21.d.0.2. | do. | ⊗ | G.27.d.0.6.to G.27.d.1.0. | do. | do. | | | |
| X. R.H.A. | G.27.a.5.9.to G.21.c.30.15. | do. | do. | Trench from South end of banks at G.21.c.4.5.to G.21.c.6.4. | zero +2'to zero +5' | 6 rds. per gun per min. | G.21.d.0.2.to G.21.d.0.6. | zero +3'to zero +45' | do. | G.27.b.0.2. to G.27.d.0.6. | Zero +45' to zero +60' | 2 rds per gun per min. |
| A./295. | G.21.c.30.15. to G.21.c.10.35. | do. | do. | Bank with dug outs at G.21.c.30.75. | zero +2'to zero +5' | do. | G.21.d.0.6.to G.21.a.9.0. | zero +5'to zero +45' | ⊗ | G.20.a.85.40. to G.20.a.7.8. | do. | do. |
| Q. R.H.A. | G.21.c.10.35 to G.20.d.90.55. | do. | do. | Trench from G.21.c.25.60 to G.21c.20.85. | zero +3' to zero +5' | do. | G.21.a.9.0.to G.21.a.55.30. | do. | ⊗ | G.20.a.7.8. to G.14.c.7.1. | do. | do. |
| B./295. | G.20.d.90.55.to G.20.d.80.85 | do. | do. | Communication trench G.20.d.85.70 to G21c.20.85. | do. | do. | G.21.a.55.30to G.20.b.9.3. | do. | ⊗ | G.14.c.7.1. to G.14.c.5.5. | do. | do. |
| A. R.H.A. | G.20.d.80.85 to G.20.b.5.1. | zero to zero +5' | do. | G.20.b.2.0.to G.20.b.9.3. | zero +5' to zero +45' | 2 rds. per gun per min | G.20.b.3.1.to G.20.a.85.40. | zero +45' to zero +60' | | Zero +5' to zero +15' Zero +15'to zero +20' Zero +20' to zero +30' | 2 rds.per gun per min. 6 rds.per gun per min. | |
| D./298 | 1 How. on tren trench junction G.21.c.25.25. | 11.p.m.1 rd every five mins. | | Defences about PEG COPSE G.21.b. | zero to zero +60' | 1 rd. per How per min | | | | Zero +20' to zero +50' Zero +30' to zero +33' Zero +33' to zero +42' Zero +42' to zero +45' | 2 rds.per gun per min 6 rds.per gun per min. 2 rds per gun per min. 6 rds per gun per min | |
| E. R.C.H.A. | SQUARE COPSE & FILLER REDOUBT | zero to zero +60' | 2 rds. per gun per min | | | | | | | | | |

Lt.Col.
For 5th.Cav. Div.Arty.

SECRET

W. Diary

## 5th. CAVALRY DIVISIONAL ARTILLERY OPERATION ORDER No. 17

Copy No........

July 9th, 17

1. When the relief of the Cavalry Corps is complete, the 34th. Divisional Artillery will cover the whole front now held by 4th. and 5th. Cavalry Div. It will be reinforced for the time being by the 16th Brigade R.H.A. on the extreme right of the 5th. Cavalry Division area.

2. Moves and reliefs will accordingly take place as in attached table.

3. 5th. Cavalry Divn. Battery Commanders will remain in command until final relief is completed on the night of the 11th/12th, when command will pass to incoming Battery Commanders.

4. All maps, kite-boards etc. will be handed over by Batteries to their relieving Batteries.

5. Existing telephone lines will be handed over intact.

6. Each night's relief will be reported to this Office when completed.

7. Battery Commanders will arrange with incoming Battery Commanders that Liaison Officers and F.O.O's of relieving Batteries shall be at their posts at 9.00.a.m. on the 11th instant, but 5th. Cavalry D.A. Liaison and F.O.O's. will not leave these posts until final relief of Batteries is notified.

8. The Medical Officer will see that all Sanitary arrangements are handed over in good order.

9. Command of Groups will pass on completion of reliefs on the night of 11th/12th July.

10. Acknowledge.

                                              Lieut. R.H.A.
                                  For 5th. Cav. Divn. Arty.

Copy No. 1. N. R.H.A.
        2. X. R.H.A.
        3. A. R.C.H.A.
        4. B. R.C.H.A.
        5. A./ 295.
        6. D./ 298.
        7. R.A. 111 Corps.
        8. H.Q., R.A. 34th Div.
        9. H.Q. 101st. Infantry Bde.
    10. 16th. Bde. R.H.A.
    11. 295th. Bde. R.F.A.         15. Q. 5th. Cav. Divn.
    12. Signal Squadron.           16. G. "   "
    13. A.D.M.S.                   17 to 20 War Diary.
    14. S.S.O.

## 4th. CAVALRY DIVISIONAL ARTILLERY RELIEF TABLE

Issued with Operation Order No.17

| Night. | Unit. | No of guns. | From. | To. | Relieving Unit. |
|---|---|---|---|---|---|
| 10th/11th. | 'M' R.H.A. | 2. | Position in Action. | Present Wagon Lines. | 'U' R.H.A. and E/152.RFA |
| do.do. | 'K' R.H.A. | 2. | do. | do. | C. / 152 R.F.A. |
| do. | 'A' R.C.H.A. | 2. | do. | do. | 'A' R.H.A. |
| do. | 'B' R.C.H.A. | 2. | do. | do. | D. / 152 R.F.A. |
| do. | D. / 298. | 2. | do. | Position near KROSSE WOOD. | do. |
| do. | A. / 295. | 2. | do. | F. 27. b. 4. 4. | A. / 152 R.F.A. |
| 11th/12th. | 'N' R.H.A. | 4. | do. | Present Wagon Lines. | 'U' R.H.A.& B/ 152 RFA |
| do. | 'K' R.H.A. | 4. | do. | do. | C. / 152 R.F.A. |
| do. | 'A' R.C.H.A. | 2. | do. | do. | 'A' R.H.A. |
| do. | 'B' R.C.H.A. | 2. | do. | do. | D. / 152 R.F.A. |
| do. | D. / 298. | 1. | do. | KROSSE WOOD. | D. / 152 R.F.A. |
| do. | A. / 295. | 4. | do. | F. 27. b. 4. 4. | A. / 152 R.F.A. |

Army Form C. 2118.

# WAR DIARY
## or
## INTELLIGENCE SUMMARY.
(Erase heading not required.)

17th Bde (?) R.H.A.

August

| Place | Date | Hour | Summary of Events and Information | Remarks and references to Appendices |
|---|---|---|---|---|
| CORONS MAX | August 1st | | Batteries in action under 2nd Canadian Divl Artillery. N. Battery R.H.A. at M.22.a.5.9 — X Battery R.H.A. at M.4.d.0.2. approximately. Offensive operation for which Batteries were brought into the Zone, postponed owing to the adverse weather conditions. | Reference Maps. Lens 1:100,000 Sheet 36 Z 1:40,000 |
| " | 3rd | | Lieut. C. West R.H.A. arrives from the Chestnut Troop R.H.A. on appointment as adj. Captain of X Battery R.H.A. | |
| " | 4th | | G.O.C., I & I 7th Cavalry Divsn. accompanied by an officer of the 5th Field Squadron R.E. visited the Battery wagon lines. | |
| " | 5th | | Major H.W. Walker MC. R.H.A. returns from leave, and resumes command of X Battery R.H.A. Lieut Gray, R.F. 17-5th Field Spadron arrives into do shopping to construct shelters for the men, latrines sheds etc., in the wagon lines. Col. Cotter CMG DSO. A.D.M.S. 2nd Cav. Divn. with O.C. Adv. visited the Battery wagon lines. | |
| " | 7th | | | |
| " | 8th | | France Heir Gen. M.G. R.A. 1st Army visited N. Battery from position. Br. General Gregory CB. Commandant Cav. Adv. visited N. Battery wagon lines. Capt. P.J. Crickman reported to Battery R.H.A. on relinquishing the temporary command of X Battery R.H.A. | |

# WAR DIARY or INTELLIGENCE SUMMARY

Army Form C. 2118.

(2)

| Place | Date | Hour | Summary of Events and Information | Remarks and references to Appendices |
|---|---|---|---|---|
| CORPS d' M.A.  | 10. | | 2Lt. G. Robinson R.H.A. - C.F.V. Macaynes R.H.A. proceeded on leave to U.K. | |
| " | 13th | | 2Lt. E.C. Mitchell R.H.A. returned from leave to U.K. | |
| " | " | | Captain J.I. Anderson R.H.A. proceeded on leave to U.K. | |
| " | 14th | | Lieut G.A. Fenton R.H.A. appt. to be actg Captain with effect from 3.8.17 GRO 2807. | |
| " | 15th | 3.0am | Attack on German trench system fifth north of hereof by Canadian Corps. All objectives in the south found by 11.00am. 1st Canadian Divn in the north held up on their final objective. The enemy made heavy counter attacks all day and into the night but were driven off. Prisoners reported by prisoners fourteen executed on 14.8.17, but confirmed. No details obtainable as to troops or definite location of our Batteries. Battery wagons and extreme had very heavy work supplying ammunition which had to be taken up in broad daylight. X Battery lost 4 horses killed during the day. One horse of X Battery was passed injured. | |
| | 16th | | Withdrawal of the 2nd South Australian Battalion Inf. Bde S. of shelling reached howitzer gun lines, and his Frenchmen. One enemy shell exploded attacking trench. | |
| | 17th | | Withdrawn from shelling in vicinity. Two prisoners (Canadian) wounded heavy and in hostile some 1600 prisoners and many machine guns were captured. The enemy lost very heavily in counter attacks. | |

# WAR DIARY
## or
## INTELLIGENCE SUMMARY.

*(Erase heading not required.)*

Army Form C. 2118.

(3)

| Place | Date | Hour | Summary of Events and Information | Remarks and references to Appendices |
|---|---|---|---|---|
| | 18ᵗʰ | | Orders were received for N & X batteries to be in readiness to join CDA. Remaining in their present positions and forming a group with the 7/439 Field Battery. Major Garrett and Major D.S.O. RHA to Headquarters Brigade H.Q. were moving to N Battery position at M.22.a.59 where also group HQ. To act between RHA (proceed) at least and 2 pieces T.A.H. Board RFA BHK was to inter-bathing of Battery adjutant of the brigade. Sergt Mostin was sent out and asked R.H. regardless to return as a discharge commensurate with the other ranks in the group. | Reference LENS 1:10,000 sheet 11 M.22.a.59 |
| | 19ᵗʰ | | Major previously mentioned to be acting adjutant proceeded to H.Q. 10ᵗʰ Canadian Infantry Brigade to discuss the situation with General Hilliam. In Col. Sage's absence 50ᵗʰ Battn Canadian Infantry, with whom this group was acting. BC went to Group HQ to receive instructions & prepare plans. 2/Lt E.A. Mitchell, N Battery RHA goes on E.O.'s to ⁺ Batt Can Inf HQ. | |

Army Form C. 2118.

# WAR DIARY
## or
## INTELLIGENCE SUMMARY.
(Erase heading not required.)

(A.)

Instructions regarding War Diaries and Intelligence Summaries are contained in F. S. Regs., Part II. and the Staff Manual respectively. Title pages will be prepared in manuscript.

| Place | Date | Hour | Summary of Events and Information | Remarks and references to Appendices |
|---|---|---|---|---|
| LIEVIN. | 20. | - | Preparations for attack on MOOF & CINNIBAR Trenches. Attack places tomorrow. | Ref. Map. Lens. 1/10,000. |
| Riaumont | 21st. | - | Our troops commenced attack on the same front, and it would appear that the enemy had about an equal preparation in attack for the same time, as their troops commenced their advance with ours, and the fighting which ensued was of a very hand to hand nature had frequently carried his line. "No man's land," being twice had frequently carried his line. Situation for a long time was obscure. First definite news of the situation received:— 4th Battalion had been gained except in the centre where we were held up in front of ALOOF, and the barrage had to be brought back accordingly. The 8th believes has been twice continuously since 3.0 am. |  |
|  |  | 9.0 am | This him the German counter attacks commenced, and |  |
|  |  | 3.1pm | Germans were reported to be massing at the junction of MOOF & DITTY TRENCHES was now shown. It was definitely established that the enemy was holding MOOF and CINNIBAR trenches prior to our attacks, and had been driven by his counter attacks. |  |

# WAR DIARY
## or
## INTELLIGENCE SUMMARY.

(Erase heading not required.)

Army Form C. 2118.

| Place | Date | Hour | Summary of Events and Information | Remarks and references to Appendices |
|---|---|---|---|---|
| Lizerne & Boesinghe | 21st | 6.40 pm | The enemy were reported to be massing in front, and M. Reinschraven telegraph intimated that the attack will commence tonight. When the attack was actually taken on the morning of 23rd, it was found to be starting with German dead. This typed of starting drew considerable fire from both the attacking infantry & many field armies. Indirect firing ceased, but most of the men were manning throughout the night, with a view to harassing the enemy. |  |
|  | 22nd | 9.7pm | T.O.P. signals went up & white fire was opened. The fire did no damage to [?] General. |  |
|  |  | Soon | Strong hostile infantry attacks were driven off when they came into the attacking infantry's sight in the most valuable information, which was practically the only information sent through during a time of great difficulty; and when the situation was critical and very obscure. This officer was extensively recommended for the Military Cross for this work. |  |
|  | 26th |  | A fresh attack in front supported by artillery fire was successful. Ammunition supply trains and men that adieu and big work had been [?]... |  |

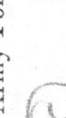

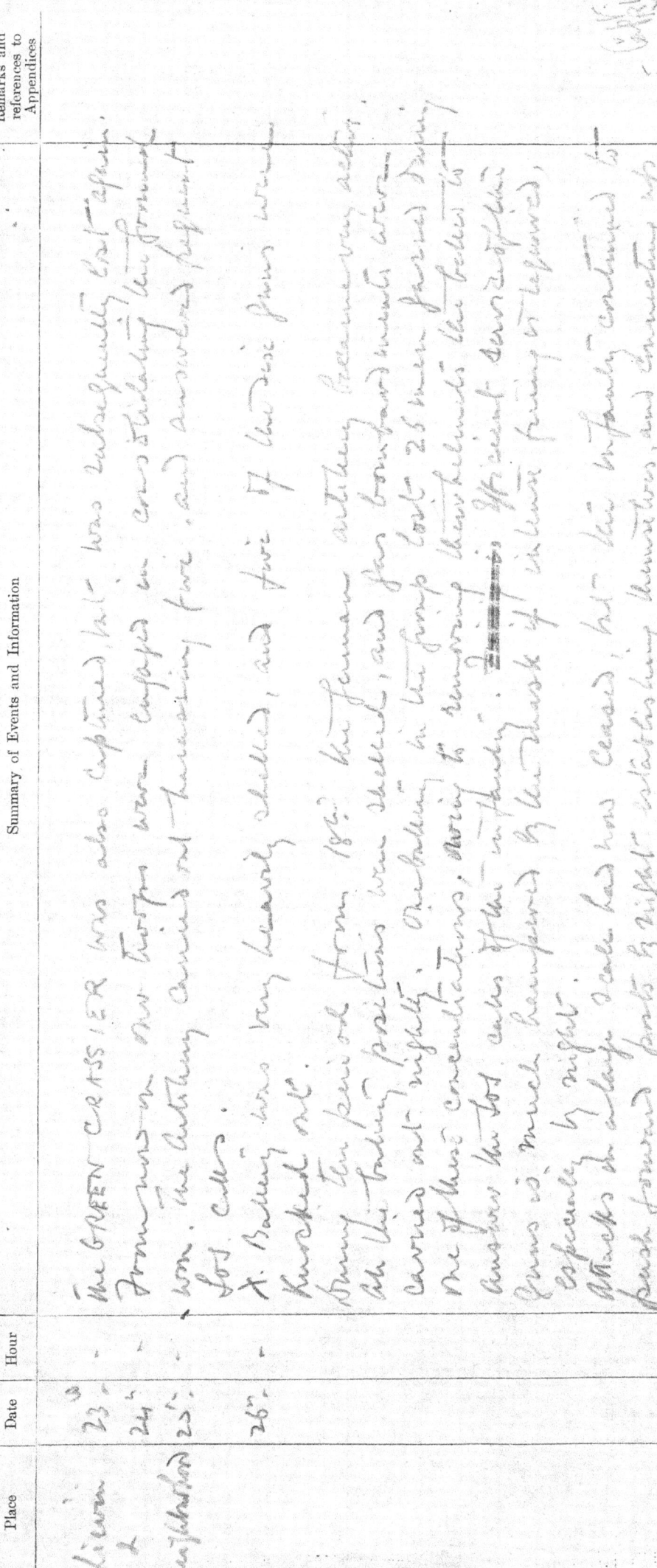

Serial No: 295

Army Form C. 2118.

**WAR DIARY**
or
**INTELLIGENCE SUMMARY**
(Erase heading not required.)

17th Bgde R.H.A.

September 1917

| Place | Date | Hour | Summary of Events and Information | Remarks and references to Appendices |
|---|---|---|---|---|
| LIEVIN | 1st | — | Lieut. W. Stewart 310 RFA returned from leave & 2/Lt W. lush rea assumed command of the Brigade from Major G.M. Thorneycroft D.S.O. R.F.A. who resumed the command of M. Battery R.H.A. | Leave 1/100 rd |
| | 2, 3 | | Considerable artillery activity on both sides. The enemy many large projectors on the Oso Lievin by night | |
| | 3 | | Capt. G.A. Fenton R.H.A. returned from leave to U.K. | |
| | 4th | | Raid on Cinnabar trench, no large raids who very successful two wounded lost — the brigade wires believed in the 6 – 7·5. Batteries of the 5th Canadian Siege Artillery Brigade (Cdos) & Gt. Ogilvy assisted today harassing fire schemes & tasking own | Gun Branch Ly 1/12 rd |
| | 5th | | | |
| | 5·6 | | positions & battery, fire lines supplied at a very heavy fire bombardment from 2 a.m. – 6·30 a.m. All worn were cut, and the tow were maintaining a continuous returning fire. Very little hostile but work was most noteworthy and our operator was times for 3·30 a.m. were undesirably carried out | |
| | 6th | | 3·30 a.m. – 8·30 a.m. German heavy artillery 8" and 5·9" shelled the vicinity of their Brunette very heavily | |

# WAR DIARY or INTELLIGENCE SUMMARY

Army Form C. 2118.

| Place | Date | Hour | Summary of Events and Information | Remarks and references to Appendices |
|---|---|---|---|---|
| LIÉVIN | 6–7 | — | Brigade relieved by 14th Batn. C.B. and withdrawn through used railway incident. | [illegible notes] |
| CAROIS d'AIX | 7 | — | Cleaning up, and preparations for tomorrows march. | |
| " | 8 | — | Brigade marched from wagon lines to the BURBURE AREA under orders 1st Army. H.Qrs. billeted for the night at Chateau LA CÔMTÉ 1 mile S. of OURTON – N×X. Relieves OURTON – Arming Column. BATUS. | |
| OURTON | 9 | — | Units marched independently to billets in the 5th Can. Divl. area. H.Q. at BERGUENEUSE. – N.Rn. at HESTRUS – K.Rn. at ABBAYE d'NEUVILLE Farm. Arming Column – La THIEULOYE. Batteries under orders of Cavalry Brigade. | |
| BERGUENEUSE | 10 | — | In billets. Resting and cleaning up. | |
| " | 11 | — | Remounts for the brigade taken over from Cavalry who had been holding operations from them. From the time of their arrival pending the relief by the Batteries. | |
| " | 12 | — | Bde R.H.A. Brev. Lt Colonel Mo. – Major Cardwyn. Lt Kerry – Ant Garden. Cmd. Backward inspected the horses of the Brigade, and about 70 horses were cast as unsuitable for horse artillery, very well fed but showing signs of hard work. | |

Army Form C. 2118.

# WAR DIARY
## or
## INTELLIGENCE SUMMARY.
*(Erase heading not required.)*

| Place | Date | Hour | Summary of Events and Information | Remarks and references to Appendices |
|---|---|---|---|---|
| BERGUENEUSE & WAVRANS | 15. | — | The Brigade Commander and Staff for Gen. Spencer's benefit and N. Rodney Rm. visited Route N reconnoitred. | |
| WAVRANS | 16. | — | Presentation of decorations to officers, N.C.O.s & men stationed in the Corps Commander's Reserves in Him Kandyk. Gen. N. Rodney took part in a field day with the Canadian Cav. Bde at | |
| do | 19. | — | which the Corps Commander was present. | |
| do | 30. | — | Individuals and Kinsmen of Squadrons in turn of Field work with the Cavalry Latelly pace daily. Regiment arrived from Merkghem (Belgium) 27th 6.30: at Start Cpt. H.Q. Lieut. Ja Mitchell & Lieut. Ca Salmon (casualties) evacuated to Etaples a staging for ever. Return from leave Cavalry Bombardier. Received under Leave Scheme — Captain PAR Barnes (B3 heavy) Major CPR Spencer Lieut Ja Rm. — Captain I Melville a 5/11 T.B Lieutenant — attached 4/12 T.B Lieut — a.f. cole was attached from Bad. Battalion when took over during the week Lieut half of 1st month. | |

Castrations Capt + Alex
JCTCS 17th Feb Pm.

Army Form C. 2118.

293

# WAR DIARY or INTELLIGENCE SUMMARY.
(Erase heading not required.)

1917 October

N⁰ Brigade R.H.A.

| Place | Date | Hour | Summary of Events and Information | Remarks and references to Appendices |
|---|---|---|---|---|
| BERGENROSE HQ. HESTRUS. N. | 1st | | Troops in test khaki. Bakery Waevey. 228 Strenuous exercises for the divisions of which in brigade Sgt. 64. | Ref. map. Lens 1:100,000 |
| Ridge & NEUVILLE X. FARM. | | | Orders received from X Battery for test exercises in readiness to proceed overseas. Bakery was accordingly made up to Establishment of horses from the remounts and have stayed. Establishment. Brs. men on leave were ordered to return at once. Bakery is informed in Establishment W.E. part VII 17 Nov. 16. Reductions of their horses, establishment were allotted in the brigade on division. A certain of horses etc. was proceeded with. The Bakery has to have extra traction. |  |
| HESTRUS. James ave. | 2nd | | Inspection of X Bakery RHA in khaki by Lieut Gregory for Commander the Bdes. Col. RHA. Cavalry Corps — General Seligman visits the place to inspect remounts, and say food etc. to X Bakery. | |
| " | 3rd | | | |
| " | 4th | | X Bakery received orders that eat. train commanders to be handed in April to reathed, and that they were to proceed forthwith. This was carried out with the assistance of the Remount C.T. & Remount Park. | |

Officers appeared with Bakery on 4th Nov :— Major Stes. Walker at R.H.A. in command. Capt. C West RHA 2nd in Cmd — 2/Lt. G.P. Sautvoord RFa. — 2/Lt. Me Phillips R9a — 2/L. A.J. Ford R9a Vet Brig? Lt. G. Robinson R9a in charge of the station of Remounts.

# WAR DIARY
## or
## INTELLIGENCE SUMMARY.
(Erase heading not required.)

Army Form C. 2118.

| Place | Date | Hour | Summary of Events and Information | Remarks and references to Appendices |
|---|---|---|---|---|
| Lumm area | 5th | | Orders received of Field X. Bailing with Indians at St Pol, on the 8th inst: being strick. off his strength from that date. | Lens. 1:100,000. |
| | 6th | | By hot division with some with Commoners. Bde. Cmdr. visits X. Bry.; B.Bry. for 14. X. Bailing for retained, and administered by 7th Corps at St Pol. The department of X. Bailing the way now coming behind of the brigade, marching with its own Cavalry brigade. Bde HQ. marching as a unit of Divisional troops into Div HQ. also detachments under orders of Reconnaissance Cav. Bde. Irony with rain marched in St HILAIRE & STEEN BECQUE, and thence for the night. | St Pol. Hazebrouck. 1:100,000 |
| STEENBECQUE | 7th | | Continued the march at 5.30am. via HAZEBROUCK, and STEENVOORDE to POPERINGHE. Nearly all the march carried out in a violent gale, and drenching rain. M. Bailing at WATOU, which was also HQ. Reconnaissance Cav Bde. The Armour Col. marching to lay behind us. | |
| POPERINGHE area | 8th | | Horses in hutments, from standing fires 7am to 9pm, when the rain started again. | |
| | 9th | | Bde. Cmdr. & Col. Wellerby DSO. R.Hse. North Canadian Corps- CAMBLAIN NABBÉ. on duty. 60 miles by motor. | Lens 1:100,000. |

Army Form C. 2118.

# WAR DIARY
## or
## INTELLIGENCE SUMMARY.
*(Erase heading not required.)*

Instructions regarding War Diaries and Intelligence Summaries are contained in F.S. Regs., Part II. and the Staff Manual respectively. Title pages will be prepared in manuscript.

(3)

| Place | Date | Hour | Summary of Events and Information | Remarks and references to Appendices |
|---|---|---|---|---|
| Serre Aryes | 16-13 Whole bat. | | In Bivouacs Overnight area known as Gr. near HAZOO. | |
| | 12th | | Lieut. R.C.L. Bart returns from leave to H.Q., and the C.V.O.O. arrives to carry out inspection of all 13 pdr. Ammn. in the division. | |
| " | 13th | | Orders received for move westwards tomorrow. | |
| " | 14th – 10:30 am | | Div. Ammn. Column move westwards. Bde. HQ. marched 10.30 am via HAZEBR- STEENVOORDE – CASSEL & RENESCURE, and billeted for the night. Ammn. Column marched afterwards, and billeted in the same village. N. Battery marching with Divisional Bde. a day behind. | Marslunselse 1 man, oro. |
| RENESCURE | 15th | | March continued at 10 am. RENESCURE via ARQUES – Southern Outskirts St OMER – WIZERNES. | |
| Boisdemer | 16th | | D.O.O. marching with the division, and continuing inspection of Ammn. Station Groote. March continued at 9.45 am. via Fauquembergues, and Fruges to RANQUES. Ammn. Col. KEROUELQ. N. Battery on move tomorrow to Fruges. Bde. HQ. at FRESSIN. March ends. 5t. Lights Ammn. Bartd. Bakery to serve village not. Camps. | Station Groote. Kew. 1 mare, oro |
| RANQUES | 17th 18th | | Training, cleaning up, refitting. | |
| Area | 19th | | X. Battery sail from Marseilles receives instructions not to pass its place for the present. | |

# WAR DIARY
## or
## INTELLIGENCE SUMMARY.

Army Form C. 2118.

| Place | Date | Hour | Summary of Events and Information | Remarks and references to Appendices |
|---|---|---|---|---|
| Same area | 20. | | C.D.O. proceeds to 4th Cav. Divn. on completion of inspection of Cameron if Lim Division. | Cameron Scot |
| " | 21.-22. | | 2 Whole training - one of hours. | |
| " | 22. | | Orders received for 9th A.M. Parade to proceed to manoeuvre ground near Bryn | |
| | | | Trog Troops in being shock the through of division. | |
| " | 23. } 24. } 28. | | 9th A.M. Parading hour division. | |
| | | | In British Command reserve. Very indifferent weather. | |
| " | 25. | | C.R.M. attends inspection of horses of the Royal Canadian Horse Artillery Brigade, and the examination of horses of the R.C.H.A. - General Innes inspects. | |
| " | 30. | | Routine work. | |
| " | 31. | | Captain G.C. Gee R.A.M.C. No. 9 the Brigade proceeds on leave to the UK. Lieut. J. Hollis By. R.F.A.(S.R.) 17 Bde. R.H.A. Cameron Brown proceeds on 6 months special leave to New Zealand, and is struck of the strength of the brigade. | |

C.C. Shelton Chapman R.H.A.
for V.C. Cavalry 17th Brigade R.H.A.
C.R.M 3rd Cav. Division

Army Form C. 2118.
295

WAR DIARY
or
INTELLIGENCE SUMMARY.
(Erase heading not required.)

5th Cav Dv
17th Brigade R.H.A.

November 1914

| Place | Date | Hour | Summary of Events and Information | Remarks and references to Appendices |
|---|---|---|---|---|
| RANQUES Area. | 1st | | In billets. Normal routine and training. | LENS 1/100,000 |
| | 2nd | | Inspection of the division by General MacAndrew. | |
| | 3rd | | Inspection of N Battery in state order by the G.R.H.A. and officers of the R.C.H.A. Brigade. | |
| FRUGES. | 5th | | Captain J.S. Anderson - N Battery RHA. Posted to the Command of Y Battery R.H.A. | |
| RANQUES | 6th | | Major G.A. Fenton - Adjt. 17 Bde. R.H.A. Posted as A.d.S. Adjutant to N Battery RHA Lt T.A.M. Bond R.F.A. - Orderly Off "" " " - Posted to Y Battery in succession to Captain Shuter, and assumes Adjt rank of Captain. News shortly received into the effect from the 8th November. Captain J.S. Anderson RHA. Bows the brigade on being to Field Artillery. | |
| " | 8th | | Orders received for 5th Cavalry Division to move South Divisional troops to march under orders of C.R.H.A. Billeted with Brer Brigade. | |
| " | 9th | | | |
| " | 10th | | Divisional troops under orders of C.R.H.A. marched to its Central Area. H.Q. 17 Bde R.H.A. billeted for the night at MEZEROLLES. | |

Army Form C. 2118.

# WAR DIARY
## or
## INTELLIGENCE SUMMARY.

Head Qrs 17th Brigade R.H.A

(Erase heading not required.)

Instructions regarding War Diaries and Intelligence Summaries are contained in F. S. Regs., Part II. and the Staff Manual respectively. Title pages will be prepared in manuscript.

| Place | Date | Hour | Summary of Events and Information | Remarks and references to Appendices |
|---|---|---|---|---|
| MEZEROLLES | 11th | | Marched with divisional troops from MEZEROLLES to QUERRIEU. | LENS 1:100,000 |
| QUERRIEU | 12th | | Marched from QUERRIEU at 4 p.m. arriving at CAPPY 9-30 p.m. Spent night at CAPPY. | ST QUENTIN 1:100,000 |
| CAPPY | 13th | | Marched from CAPPY at 3-30 p.m. arriving at BOUVINCOURT about 9 p.m. N.Battery at BOURLES. A.Battery R.C.H.A. at CARTIGNY with incessible Brigade. B.Battery R.C.H.A. at HAMELET. R.H.A. & R.C.H.A ammunition blowned at ESTREES. H.Q. 17th Bde R.H.A at BOUVINCOURT with divnl. H.Q. | |
| BOUVINCOURT | 14th | | Getting united in at BOUVINCOURT. | |
| " | 15th | | Information received of proposed offensive by Cavalry Corps. Busy making preparations. Lt.Col. W. Sterling A.V.O. R.H.A went to 3rd Corps H.Q. to ascertain artillery preparations. | |
| " | 16th | | at Bouvincourt. busy with plans & preparations for forthcoming operations. | |
| " | 17th | | Conference at divisional H.Q. at which C.R.H.A and adjutant were present. Scheme for forthcoming operations outlined and discussed. Busy with preparations. Capt E.C. GELL R.A.M.C. returned from leave | |

Army Form C. 2118.

# WAR DIARY
## or
## INTELLIGENCE SUMMARY.
*(Erase heading not required.)*

| Place | Date | Hour | Summary of Events and Information | Remarks and references to Appendices |
|---|---|---|---|---|
| Gouzeaucourt | 17th | | The object of the operations now in course of preparation were briefly as follows: The enemy's line was to be attacked by us on a 12 mile front from a point east of GONNELIEU to a point east of HERLY. The attack was to be a complete surprise. The main feature being that a body of 380 tanks were to be relied on to beat the enemy's wire defences & that there was to be no artillery preparation. The object of the attack was to break the enemy's defences by a coup de main 9 to push the cavalry thro' the breach thus formed. The cavalry were then to work in the direction of CAMBRAI with the intention of isolating CAMBRAI from the N. N.E. & East. The rôle of the 5th Cavalry Division was to advance on parallel lines towards MASNIÈRES and MARCOING to cross the canal at l'ESCAUT at these points & then to work N.E. thro RUMILLY — NIERGNES — ANSIGNY & on around the SENSÉE river. The rôle of the cavalry will not begin till the infantry & tanks have (presumably) the enemy's defences & made a path for them. The 1st & 5th Cavalry Divisions will be the first to operate. The 2nd & 4th to be followed by the 3rd | Entries & Maps [illegible] Sketch 2 |

# WAR DIARY
## or
## INTELLIGENCE SUMMARY.
*(Erase heading not required.)*

Army Form C. 2118.

War Diary 17th Bde R.H.A

| Place | Date | Hour | Summary of Events and Information | Remarks and references to Appendices |
|---|---|---|---|---|
| BOURNONVILLE | Nov. 18th | | Adjutant went on reconnaissance to forward concentration area at FINS. | |
| | | | Preparations complete for forthcoming operations. | |
| | | | The head quarter staff of the Brigade will go in to action as follows: | |
| | | | In Group 2. of Divisional H.Qrs.   Lt.Col. W. Herbing DSO. R.H.A | |
| | | | Capt. T.A.J. Evans    Adjutant | |
| | | | 2nd Philips  ?   orderlies | |
| | | | Gunner Whitley | |
| | | |  | |
| | 19th | | In Group III.  Fighting troops | |
| | | | Sergt. E. Martin    A/Bmbr Webb    Gnr. Campbell    Bmbr. Conway |
| | | | Bmbr. Doughty    Gnr. Evans    Gnr. Rainard    S.S. Farrell |
| | | | Gnr. Buckley    Gnr. Alphick    Gnr. Clarkson    A/M. Rodwell |
| | | | Gnr. Stevens    Gnr. Eastmure    Gnr. Grey    2nd A/M. Dellaway |
| | | |  | |
| | | | N.C.O. in charge of Telephone cart    Cpl. Harry ball | |
| | | | Drivers of Telephone cart.   D. Newcombe   D. Smith | |
| | | |   "   "   L.G.S.    D. Hill    D. Allen | |
| | | |  Gunners.    D. Walker    D. Taylor    D. Burrell | |

Army Form C. 2118.

# WAR DIARY
## or
## INTELLIGENCE SUMMARY.
(Erase heading not required.)

Instructions regarding War Diaries and Intelligence Summaries are contained in F. S. Regs., Part II. and the Staff Manual respectively. Title pages will be prepared in manuscript.

| Place | Date | Hour | Summary of Events and Information | Remarks and references to Appendices |
|---|---|---|---|---|
| | Nov | | | ST QUENTIN |
| BOUVINCOURT | 19th | | No 2 A Echelon. | VALENCIENNES 1:100,000 |
| | | | MGN cart. M. Beesley. M. Tessier | |
| | | | Maltese cart. Pte Hopton | |
| | | | L.F.S. wagon N. Howell. M. Hartwig | |
| | | | B echelon. E.S. wagon. D. Wilson. M. Pallan. | |
| | | | with Amm. Col. Sergt. Colley. Bm. Hogues. Lester. French. Gm. Mack. | |
| | | | The batteries in the 5th Cavalry Divisions were as under: | |
| | | | N Battery R.H.A. with the Lucerna Bde Cavalry Brigade | |
| | | | A Battery R.C.H.A. with the Seaforths Cavalry Brigade | |
| | | | B Battery R.C.H.A. with the Canadian Cavalry Brigade | |
| | | | Right section Jmies. Their batteries on the 19th morning | |
| | | | The M.O. Capt. E. Gell. R.A.M.C. with his Quarters Nr. Bouvenas | |
| | | | Junes the Ammunition Column fewer this H.Q. this day | |
| | | | information was received this morning Ref the Armistice will | |

# WAR DIARY or INTELLIGENCE SUMMARY.

Army Form C. 2118.

Instructions regarding War Diaries and Intelligence Summaries are contained in F. S. Regs., Part II. and the Staff Manual respectively. Title pages will be prepared in manuscript.

(Erase heading not required.)

| Place | Date | Hour | Summary of Events and Information | Remarks and references to Appendices |
|---|---|---|---|---|
| BOUVINCOURT | Nov. 19th | | march to the forward concentration area at FINS to-night & that XIII day will be to-morrow. The 20th west | ST. QUENTIN VALENCIENNES 1:100,000 |
| | 20th | | "B" Brigade & 11th H.Q. left BOUVINCOURT at 12.45 a.m. with groups 2 & 3 of Divisional H.Q. FINS was reached about 6.30 a.m. on the 20th after a tedious march in the dark & units proceeded to the areas allotted to them to behind DESSART wood horses being watered & fed. The infantry & tank attack commenced at 6.20 a.m. heavy firing being heard. The weather was very misty & foggy. Quite impossible for any air reconnaissance. No news of our plans were up. The 5th Cavalry Division was(?) in the forward area, saddles up & ready to move at a moment's notice, until about 12 noon. The Canadian Cavalry Brigade then moved off followed by Lee'bes Cavalry Brigade, Divisional H.Q. with an escort of two troops of Yorkshire Dragoons finally moving out of behind Lee'bes Brigade at 12.30 p.m. followed by Lucknow Brigade, & advanced thro' GOUZEAUCOURT & VILLERS PLOUICH towards MARCOING. A good many German prisoners were seen & there was evidence that | |

Army Form C. 2118.

# WAR DIARY or INTELLIGENCE SUMMARY.

(Erase heading not required.)

| Place | Date | Hour | Summary of Events and Information | Remarks and references to Appendices |
|---|---|---|---|---|
|  | Nov 20th |  | The enemy had been taken completely by surprise & has abandoned the main strong defences of the HINDENBURG line in considerable haste & disorder. | Enemy reconnaissance Map Sheet 2 57b & 57c. |
|  |  | 2.30 p.m. | Divisional H.Q. reached the plateau about R.9 central about 2.30 p.m. & Report centre was opened there. Canadian Cavalry Brigade was then advancing on MASNIÈRES to establish line in R.5 -- The two cavalry Brigades advancing on MARCOING in L.27 & 28. Lucknow Brigade in reserve. The 7th D.G's afterwards reported MARCOING clear & the bridge over the canal intact. Eventually the infantry were held up by the MASNIÈRES-BEAUREVOIR line & H.Q. advanced squadrons of Cavalry crossed the canal. They were unable to maintain themselves there. One squadron of the 7th D.G's were reported to be in NOYELLES at 8.55 p.m. Divisional H.Q. eventually decided not to move that night. The two Cavalry Brigades were withdrawn across the canal & a very cold night was spent in the open under cover, keeping communication. |  |

Army Form C. 2118.

# WAR DIARY or INTELLIGENCE SUMMARY.
(Erase heading not required.)

H.Q. 17th Brigade R.H.A.

Instructions regarding War Diaries and Intelligence Summaries are contained in F.S. Regs., Part II. and the Staff Manual respectively. Title pages will be prepared in manuscript.

| Place | Date | Hour | Summary of Events and Information | Remarks and references to Appendices |
|---|---|---|---|---|
| Between VILLERS PLUICH and MARCOING | 21st | | The morning was spent in writing for difficulty news & hoping that a further advance would still be possible. The weather continued misty & foggy & there was a marked absence of enemy artillery activity on the sector on which 5th Cav. Divnl. H.Q. lay - most of the firing seemed to be going on our left flank. | Enemy post Masnières Sheet 2. 57c & 57b. |
| | | 1pm | 5th Cavalry Bde reports on receipt of information that our infantry has taken the MASNIÈRES - BEUVREVOIR line. Canadian Cavalry Brigade was ordered to cross the canal at MASNIÈRES to secure the high ground between NIERGNIES and SERANVILLERS at the moment the Canadian Cavalry Brigade was debouching from MASNIÈRES heavy hostile counter attack from the direction of NIERGNIES took place and prevented further forward movement of the Brigade. | |
| | | 2.30 1pm | 5.A. Cav. Arv. was ordered to place AMB R.H.A. Cavalry Brigade at the disposal of the 1st Cav. Div. forthwith. K.A. Othered Cartg. R.C.H.A. Brigade and A. Battery R.C.H.A. went with the Brigade Lt. Col. W. Stirling DSO. R.H.A. went to H.Q. 29th R.H.A. Brigade. | |

Army Form C. 2118.

# WAR DIARY or INTELLIGENCE SUMMARY.

(Erase heading not required.)

11 Oct 17th August R.H.A.

| Place | Date | Hour | Summary of Events and Information | Remarks and references to Appendices |
|---|---|---|---|---|
| Between VILLERS-PLOUICH & MARCOING | Noon. 21st | | Artillery to try & close up the situation. | Ensuing map movement sheet 2. 57C + 57b |
| | | 5.17 p.m. | The situation of the Cavalry Corps Brigade was as follows: 1 Regiment & 1 battery - L 36 c. Brigade less 1 regiment - C 26 c. | |
| | | 11.45 p.m. | 5th Cavalry Division were ordered to withdraw on the morning of the 22nd inst to the FINS area. | |
| | | | Horses & men had been on the ground since they left Bourincourt at about midnight on the 19th. There was very little water in the vicinity of VILLERS-PLOUICH & horses were very badly watered once on the 20th & twice on the 21st. The eight hour agreement of the men on the batteries. | |
| | 22nd 7.30 a.m. | | The 5th Cavalry Division withdrew to EQUINCOURT, & 15 echelons & ammunition columns remaining at FINS from which they had not moved since their arrival on the morning of the 20th. None of the batteries had (even) a period, but all must have a time of considerable fatigue & discomfort with cheerful appearance city | |

Army Form C. 2118.

# WAR DIARY
## or
## INTELLIGENCE SUMMARY.
(Erase heading not required.)

11 Oric. 17th August R.H.A.

Instructions regarding War Diaries and Intelligence Summaries are contained in F. S. Regs., Part II. and the Staff Manual respectively. Title pages will be prepared in manuscript.

| Place | Date | Hour | Summary of Events and Information | Remarks and references to Appendices |
|---|---|---|---|---|
| EQUANCOURT | 23rd | | and hoped that chance was yet to come. As far as can be ascertained, the 7th DGs & Fort Garry Horse were the only units of the division which really had any opportunity of cavalry action & a squadron of the latter particularly has been fighting dis-mounted somewhat front lines. The night of the 22nd was spent in EQUANCOURT | |
| | 23rd 8.40am | | The division marched to SUZANNE via ETRICOURT - MANANCOURT MOISLAINS - ALLAINES - CLERY - MARICOURT - Rackery SUZANNE about 1-30 p.m. The divisions received no orders to move or again at that notice while the march was made up the time available to get things straight, clean, agreed. The horses had stood the hard work and hugely laborious excellently At SUZANNE Br. CAMMELL R.F.A. joined the Brigade & came to H.Q. as orderly officer. The division is ordered to move at one hours notice. | VALENCIENNES 1:100,000<br>AMIENS 1:100,000 |

Army Form C. 2118.

# WAR DIARY
or
# INTELLIGENCE SUMMARY.
(Erase heading not required.)

| Place | Date | Hour | Summary of Events and Information | Remarks and references to Appendices |
|---|---|---|---|---|
| SUZANNE | Mar. 26th | 9 p.m. | Orders were received for the Division to march on 27th inst. to MONCHY LAGACHE | |
| | 27th | 8.15am | Divisional troops marching with the Division of C.R.H.A. Marched to MONCHY LAGACHE arriving about 4 p.m. going into bivouac | ST QUENTIN 1:100,000 |
| MONCHY LAGACHE | 28th | | Busy preparing to take over the LE VERGUIER sector at the line found by 24th Div. Division is supposed to be going in on the night of the 2nd/3rd April. | |
| | 30th | 9 a.m. | Headquarters reopening at MONCHY LAGACHE. Warning received for Division to be ready to move at half an hour's notice. | |
| | | 9.30am | Orders received for Division to ready-move at once at X roads E. of EPÉHY. Bde - CHANGÉ. R.E. Artillery R.F.C. & R.H.A. & Cycl. Coys accordingly. Later the orders to meet the Divisional Commander at the rendezvous were cancelled. Information received that the enemy had attacked in force on the CAMBRAI front and broken thro' the 59th Division, penetrating as far as la VACQUERIE & GOUZEAUCOURT and VILLERS GUISLAINS cavalry to be moved up to counter attack. The 5th Cavalry Division moved on at once to VILLERS-FAUCON and thence in the direction of VILLERS GUISLAINS between HEUDICOURT and EPEHY | |

# WAR DIARY
## INTELLIGENCE SUMMARY.
*(Erase heading not required.)*

Army Form C. 2118.

| Place | Date | Hour | Summary of Events and Information | Remarks and references to Appendices |
|---|---|---|---|---|
| | 30.11.17 | 3 pm | It was decided to attack at once in the hope of clearing the enemy out of VILLERS GUISLAIN and GONNELIEU. "B" Batty went with the "BAD" Brigade to GOUZEAUCOURT. "A" Battery in RESERVE. GUISLAIN held down but the enemy's advance was checked. Bn. H.Q. remained about 800 x S. of JACQUELINE COPSE a wet cold night was spent in the open having both a fire further north but little shelling on our front. The Ambulances in the Brigade. "A" Batty R.C.H.A. with Ambala B? "B" R.C.H.A with Can. Cav. Bde. | |

T.O.M. Burns
Capt.
for CRHA S. Westons
12.12.17

Army Form C. 2118.

293

# WAR DIARY
## or
## INTELLIGENCE SUMMARY.
(Erase heading not required.)

December 1917

| Place | Date | Hour | Summary of Events and Information | Remarks and references to Appendices |
|---|---|---|---|---|
| H.Q. 17th Bde R.H.A. | Dec. 1st | | In action in front of VILLERS GUISLAIN. "A" Battery R.C.H.A. with Arrass Cav. Bde. which was ordered to advance with the object of retaking BON DE GAUCHE and hence GONNELIEU. "B" Batty RCHA with Can. Cav. Bde. "N" Batty R.H.A. with Fitz Gd Cav. Bde. Batteries were ready to be ready at dawn on 1st to support a tank attack on Bon EPEHINE and VILLERS GUISLAIN from positions roughly in squares 12 & 18 (GOUZEAUCOURT Map). F.O.O. "N" Batty reported after the attack had begun at 2.30 p.m. that we held GUICHE WOOD from S.W. corner to S x 7 central. Attack on VILLERS GUISLAIN failed. Batteries leaving killed during the afternoon from 3 p.m. till 9pm. "N" Batty Rt CASSELL of RCHA Bre wounded Regt. and 12 men at Lt. PENNIKE and Lt CASSELL of RCHA Bre wounded also 12 O.R. of R.C.H.A Bde. Fairly quiet night. | ref A.B. |
| | 2nd | | Artillery demonstration under C.Col. L. E. Meloney Dso R.F.A. Lt. & 3rd Can Div responsible for shelling the gaps between 7th, 4, 5th Corps C.R.H.A. ordered to cover the roller like by 5th Can Div Enemy artillery activity not nearly so heavy great day | |

2353 Wt. W2544/1454 700,000 5/15 D. D. & L. A.D.S.S./Forms/C. 2118.

# WAR DIARY or INTELLIGENCE SUMMARY.

(Erase heading not required.)

Army Form C. 2118.

| Place | Date | Hour | Summary of Events and Information | Remarks and references to Appendices |
|---|---|---|---|---|
| | Dec 2nd | 6 p.m. | 5th Cav. Div. relieved but 17th Bde R.H.A. & R.C.H.A. Brigade remained in action. "A", "Q" & "D" Batteries were grouped with 5th Can. Div. artillery under Lt Col. W. Stirling. D.S.O. R.H.A. covering the sector held by the 2nd Can. Brigade. Col. Stirling conferred with B.G. Maher & Col. Duncan. | |
| | 3rd 4th 5th | | In action in the same place. Lt Lawson R.C.H.A. Bde was wounded on 3rd but otherwise no casualties. Very little activity on this sector of the front. | |
| | 6th | 5.30pm | 17th Bde & R.C.H.A. Brigade relieved by the artillery of the III & VII Corps. Batteries relieving their Brigade. "N" to E 14 C. "A", "B" to Rouel H.Q. to Longavesnes. With the exception of the afternoon of the 1st, our 1st and 2nd recent casualties were sustained and this somewhat remarkable considering that 7 days were spent in the open more or less under direct enemy observation and south all 3 batteries firing at a range of less than 8000*. Information regarding the literature | |

# WAR DIARY or INTELLIGENCE SUMMARY

Army Form C. 2118.

was extremely difficult to obtain, but it seems that the 3rd Cavalry Divn. did valuable work in preventing the enemy advance at a time when the situation was serious as the enemy had broken through our line, penetrating as far as GAUCHE WOOD VILLERS GUISLAIN VAUCELETTE FARM and GOUZEAUCOURT.

During this week men & horses were actively on the go exposed to severe winter weather, and the spirit and moral of all ranks was admirable throughout.

17th Bugade H.Q. did its share in keeping out and maintaining communication to batteries under difficulties. The arrangements made for the supply of rations and forage were inadequate, and at times in short retained. With no regs used batteries were at times in short rations. Both men & horses have borne the strain available for the horses. It must be remembered they had been continually on well. Tho' it must be remembered they had been continually on the move since the 9th Novr.

# WAR DIARY
## or
## INTELLIGENCE SUMMARY
(Erase heading not required.)

Army Form C. 2118.

| Place | Date | Hour | Summary of Events and Information | Remarks and references to Appendices |
|---|---|---|---|---|
| | 6th | | MSV requires that Batteries to withdraw huge option as MS supply their own Key Battery positions. He suggested the Kings Bey of Brn. as GH at HQ. marched at 6 P.M. to LONGAVESNES | |
| | 7th | | Batteries with Brigades - A & B. R.H.A. at ROISEL. "N" at with their light vehicles which has been with them twice. J.B.H. Gun at LONGAVESNES. Orders received for the artillery to go in to the line on the night 8th/9th to assist in the defence of the MIDENCOURT - LE VERGIER sector. Lt. Col. Sterling visited H.Q. 24th Div. at NEUROCOURT FARM for conference. | Ans 6th 9.05 |
| | 8th | | Lt. Col. Sterling & adjutant proceeded at 10 a.m. to H.Q. Cavalry Divisional Artillery at ——————— subsequently, after conferring with C.R.A. 24th Div. and C.R.H.A. 3rd Cav. Div. Established H.O.s at Batteries moved at night in to the following positions:- "N" 4 guns at R 9 c 38      2 at R 4 d 52  "A" 4 guns at R 16 c 37   "B" 2 guns at R 4 d 70     2 guns at R 15 a 88 | |

# WAR DIARY
## or
## INTELLIGENCE SUMMARY.

Army Form C. 2118.

| Place | Date | Hour | Summary of Events and Information | Remarks and references to Appendices |
|---|---|---|---|---|
| | Nov. 8th | | Group H.Q. at R 14 b 4 9. Waggon lines at valley between POEUILLY and SOYECOURT. Main échelons at ATHIES. Right section with batteries. | Phot: b2 c9E |
| | 9th | | Arrangements completed for the formation of the Cavalry Divisional Artillery Group covering the advance in the VADENCOURT - LE VERGIER roads in conjunction with part of the 2nd No. 2nd Cav. Dy. The group was commanded by Lt Col WAINWRIGHT C.R.H.A. 3rd Cav. Div. and divided in to the following sub groups: |  |
| | | | Lt Col Makins' Group | |
| | | | "N" R.H.A. | |
| | | | U R.H.A. | |
| | | | "A" ] R.C.H.A. | |
| | | | "B" ] R.C.H.A. | |
| | | | with D/106 R.F.A. 24th Div Artillery attached. | |
| | | | Lt Col Harting's Group | |
| | | | D R.H.A. | |
| | | | E R.H.A. | |
| | | | I R.H.A. | |
| | | | Q R.H.A. | |
| | | | Major Woollcombe's Group | |
| | | | C R.H.A. | |
| | | | G R.H.A. | |
| | | | K R.H.A. | |
| | | | A R.H.A. | |

# WAR DIARY
## or
## INTELLIGENCE SUMMARY.

Army Form C. 2118.

(Erase heading not required.)

| Place | Date | Hour | Summary of Events and Information | Remarks and references to Appendices |
|---|---|---|---|---|
| | Nov 9th 1917 | | The whole of the artillery forming the Cavalry Divisional Artillery Group in covering the front held by the dismounted cavalry divisions, which runs from HETTY POST (L.18.a.30.) to a little South of RIVER POST (M.8.c.50). | map 1:20000 62C SE + NE |
| | Nov 10th | | Right Battalion with HQ at R.11.C.39 covered by the Leics Yeo. Busy all day with Engineers supplying building materials for batteries, wiring, put defence schemes &c. Quiet day and night, very little hostile activity, tho' a great number of enemy observation balloons were up, coupled with a good deal of aeroplane activity. Batteries carried out registration. | |
| | 11th | | Lt. CAMPBELL R.H.A. (orderly officer) was attached to N Battery R.H.A. who were short of officers. Capt. G.A. FENTON R.H.A. having proceeded on a Battery Commanders & Bombers course of gunnery on 7th inst. Lt. R.W. Floyd being on leave and 2/Lt. J.B. Smith having gone on a Cavalry Corps Equitation course. | |

# WAR DIARY
## or
## INTELLIGENCE SUMMARY.
(Erase heading not required.)

Army Form C. 2118.

| Place | Date | Hour | Summary of Events and Information | Remarks and references to Appendices |
|---|---|---|---|---|
| | Nov. 11th | | In the report all batteries are at present Northwards as in addition to the officers of N Battery RHA mentioned above in the RCHA Report, Lt Col. Elkins Lt Col. Lawson were both wounded and invalided and Lt Thackeray Lt Puckle and Lt Thackeray [?] in hospital. The fact that N & B batteries has Journies relieves couples with Battery & Group F.O.O. duties & various duties throws a heavy strain on the officers available. | |
| | 12th | | U Battery RHA moved to put a Relieve Journies at R.S.B.C. to carry out night Journies, as enemy relief & repairs on night. | |
| | 14/15 15/16 | | | |
| | 15th | | Lt Col W Ithelburg D.S.O. R.H.A. assumed command of Cavalry Divisional Artillery Group, as Lt Col. C.A. Wansley of Lt RHA appeared to duties at C.R.A. 2nd Div. while Lt GOC 2nd Div. was on leave. Major G.M. Spencer-Smith D.S.O. R.H.A. assumed command of Itheburg's Group | |
| | 16th | | 2/Lieut Millard & 2/Lt Coard RFA arrived & were posted to | |

2353 Wt. W2544/1454 700,000 5/15 D.D.&L. A.D.S.S./Forms/C. 2118.

Army Form C. 2118.

# WAR DIARY
## or
## INTELLIGENCE SUMMARY.
(Erase heading not required.)

Instructions regarding War Diaries and Intelligence Summaries are contained in F. S. Regs., Part II. and the Staff Manual respectively. Title pages will be prepared in manuscript.

| Place | Date | Hour | Summary of Events and Information | Remarks and references to Appendices |
|---|---|---|---|---|
| | Nov 16th | | "N" Battery R.H.A. and "B" Battery R.C.H.A. repeatedly shelled being shot by 311th Field Artillery Bregus. Heavy snowfall. | sheet 62C S.E. |
| | 17th | | Composite Horse battery (4.5") consisting of one section of D/311 and one section of D/311 (Army Field Artillery Brigade) under the command of Major Roy Rqr. relieved in Virtury's Gp. | |
| | 18th | | Major G.M. Pearce — with D+O R.H.A. proceeded to Cavalry Corps for duty as Staff Officer R.H.A. Major A. Rusby the Chesnut Troop R.H.A. assumed command of Virtury's S.A.B. Group. | |
| | 19th & th | | Two sections with battery w.d. wrote N Battery wagon lines moves to TREFCON on 19th "A" + "B" Battery R.C.H.A. wagon lines moves to CAVRINCOURT on 21st. Communication between sections reduced to March by LAGACHE. No incident of any importance occurring in the front. "V" Battery's forward section war established to the new battery position on the 23rd covering only relief of N/R.H.A. B/R.C.H.A. forward section was covered. A relieve movement of everything was done by | |

# WAR DIARY
## or
## INTELLIGENCE SUMMARY.
*(Erase heading not required.)*

Army Form C. 2118.

| Place | Date | Hour | Summary of Events and Information | Remarks and references to Appendices |
|---|---|---|---|---|
| | 30th | | New guns but visibility was very poor and little movement was shewn. Positions for defence of Potizieres and forward lines were reconnoitred and reported on. On 31st N.V.B. CAMMELL O.C. was posted to N. Battery R.H.A. and LtCol. PYE was attached to the same Battery pour se instruire at Colincamps. Cavalry Divisional Artillery is grouped at follows from 10 am on 30th H.Q. (Lt.Col. A.R. Harendorf R.H.A.) at ROSSIGNOL FT Right Group (R.R. Col. W. Hickey D/O R.H.A) Headquarters sitting at RSA & J. consisting of N.U/R.H.A, A/B/R.H.A, D/31 STRING'S sub-group D.E.F.G; A/R.H.A Mellors sub-group Left Group (Lt.Col. G.R. Hamilton R?? consisting of SCARLETT's sub-group Hamilton's sub-group The Right group covers the 3rd dismounted Bde The left group covers the 2nd dismounted division. | 82 c S.E. |

T.A.M. Andrews Capt.
for Lt.Col. comg 17th Bde R.H.A

Army Form C. 2118.

295

# WAR DIARY
# INTELLIGENCE SUMMARY.
(Erase heading not required.)

Instructions regarding War Diaries and Intelligence Summaries are contained in F. S. Regs., Part II. and the Staff Manual respectively. Title pages will be prepared in manuscript.

Headquarters
17th Brigade R.H.A.

| Place | Date | Hour | Summary of Events and Information | Remarks and references to Appendices |
|---|---|---|---|---|
| Nr VENDELLES | January 1st 1918 | | In action in the VADENCOURT - LEVERGIES sector. Lt. Col. W. Halsey D.S.O. and H.Qrs. 17th Brigade R.H.A. form the Right Group of Cavalry Divisional Artillery. The Right Group consists of Millicent sub-group & Halsey's sub-group. Millicent sub-group: D/E.H.A., E/R.H.A., T/R.H.A., Q/R.H.A., A/R.H.A. Halsey sub-group: N/R.H.A., U/R.H.A., A/R.C.H.A., B/R.C.H.A., D/311 R.F.A. | Bt. Maj. & MACROY SMITH |
| | 4th | | Lt. Col. A. Millar D.S.O. took over command of Right Group from Lt. Col. W. Halsey D.S.O. the latter proceeding on leave. T. & Q. Batteries went on to mobile reserve to their wagon lines. | |
| | 10th | | D/R.H.A. was withdrawn to form the R.H.A. reserve at VILLERS-CARBONEL. Construction of mined dug outs & 3 new battery positions for its defence of the Intermediate Line were commenced. | |
| | 14th | | Bt. Col. H.F. Filiquean D.S.O. vacates Right Group. Weather during the first half of January was cold - the lines |

# WAR DIARY
## INTELLIGENCE SUMMARY.
*(Erase heading not required.)*

Army Form C. 2118.

| Place | Date | Hour | Summary of Events and Information | Remarks and references to Appendices |
|---|---|---|---|---|
| | 1st–14th May 1918 | | continuing to be thick on the ground. Visibility was poor & activity limited to the forward guns of B/RCHA, N/RHA & J/RHA with the exception of harassing fire on the target it to 10/11th when an enemy relief was suspected, and some retaliation on the 12th for the shelling of KEVERCHE. Enemy artillery activity was also slight. A good deal of work was done in improving existing batteries positions, building new ones and constructing more dug outs. Plans were also prepared for the defence of the Reutoinhalte line. Nothing of special interest occurred. Capt. H.K. Power 17th Rugate R.H.A. Ammunition Column and Capt. F.K. Dickinson formerly of N/R.H.A. were awarded the Military Cross in the New Year's Honours List. | Ref. map Sheet 62d SE M36501 Special sheet |
| | 14th November | | No unusual incident occurred. The fire was kept up improving existing Battery positions and building new positions & mixing deep cuts for the permanent defence of | |

2353 Wt. W2514/1454 700,000 5/15 D. D. & L. A.D.S.S./Forms/C. 2118.

Army Form C. 2118.

# WAR DIARY
## INTELLIGENCE SUMMARY.
*(Erase heading not required.)*

The Battery is here. Instructed for anti-tank gun role, also constructs Tu 311th AFA Pok-[?] AIRHA E/RHA and VIRHA on the 15th inst — there Batteries going went in to mobile reserve. The front is a whole was quick throughout the period under review. 7000) forgone was most intensive. Enemy were different.

Major E.M. Spencer-Smith D/O. E/RHA proceeded on leave to the U.K. on 28th inst. Keenway Capt. E.A. Fenton to commence N/RHA

Lt. Col. Allardyce D/O. F/RHA relieved Lt. Col. A. Naster D/O R/HA in command of the Right Group on the 29th inst. Capt. T.O.M. Burns proceeded on leave on the 29th inst. K.O.B. Crommell N/RHA acting as adjutant during the absence

Orders received on Jan 30th to be held in readiness proceed to Egypt.

H. Campbell RHA

2353  Wt. W2544/1454  700,000  5/15  D. D. & L.  A.D.S.S./Forms/C. 2118.

# WAR DIARY or INTELLIGENCE SUMMARY

Army Form C. 2118.

17th Bde RHA

February 1916

| Place | Date | Hour | Summary of Events and Information | Remarks and references to Appendices |
|---|---|---|---|---|
| Meteren Billet | 2nd | | Routine training and lectures as per syllabus attached. | |
| | | | N/RHA and B/RHA Concentrated at St. Jans Cappel on the right bank of the river | |
| | | | R.W.B. Lieutenant [illegible] and of the Battery relieved and returned to [illegible] | |
| | | | In relief of Capt. John Bong on 1st in command of B/RHA was relieved. | |
| | | | Capt. O A Forster R.H.A. recommended to the command of B/RHA | |
| | | | Major F.M. [illegible] [illegible] D.S.O. as [illegible] command of | |
| | | | [illegible] [illegible] [illegible] [illegible] [illegible] | |
| | | | [illegible] [illegible] [illegible] [illegible] [illegible] | |
| | 5th | | R.W.B. [illegible] [illegible] R.H.A. [illegible] [illegible] [illegible] | |
| | | | command of B/ Brigade | |
| | 6th | | R.Col. A. Fleming took over [illegible] command of [illegible] | |
| | | | [illegible] [illegible] D.S.O. & R.H.A. | |
| | 6-20 | | The remainder of the month was [illegible] [illegible] [illegible] [illegible] [illegible] | |

Army Form C. 2118.

# WAR DIARY
or
## INTELLIGENCE SUMMARY.
(Erase heading not required.)

Instructions regarding War Diaries and Intelligence Summaries are contained in F.S. Regs., Part II. and the Staff Manual respectively. Title pages will be prepared in manuscript.

| Place | Date | Hour | Summary of Events and Information | Remarks and references to Appendices |
|---|---|---|---|---|
| | Feb. K/A 12/13 | 12.16 am | A raid was carried out by the Canadian Mounted Brigade – 200 horses being 12.16 am on the night 12/13 February 1916. The raid was carried out by the Royal Canadian Dragoons assisted by one troop of Lord Strathcona's Horse in covering party, Right Rear Guard of three troops from Lord Strathcona's Horse, and Left Flank Guard by one troop from the Fort Garry Horse. The operation was divided into several preliminary moves, from E.37 c 51 to E.20.d 80 and covering heavy shoots on E.21.c. The raiding party was assisted by a barrage from the Right Group Cavalry Divisional Artillery ensure the encasing up of the X/W Battery D.1.0 R.H.A. The batteries placed at his disposal consisted of X/R.H.A. A.D.V.U., E, Y/R.H.A., H, Y & F/R.H.A., A, B/R.CH.A., 3/1 A.F.A. Brigade and D/160 — twelve 13 p. batteries, 3/18 p. howitzers and 2 4.5 how batteries. The services of two Field batteries were also lent by the 5th Aus Inf Bde and right Cavalry | Necessary Precaution |

# WAR DIARY
# INTELLIGENCE SUMMARY.
*(Erase heading not required.)*

Army Form C. 2118.

Instructions regarding War Diaries and Intelligence Summaries are contained in F. S. Regs., Part II. and the Staff Manual respectively. Title pages will be prepared in manuscript.

| Place | Date | Hour | Summary of Events and Information | Remarks and references to Appendices |
|---|---|---|---|---|
|  | Feb 12/13 |  | Corps Heavy Artillery also participated, to that the enemy assembly was exceptionally heavy. The enemy wire was cut by the firing of a Bangalore Torpedo fired by a party of the RCD's, unfortunately the firing of the torpedo was too by the "Y" gun for Zero hour — 12.16 a.m. on night 12/13th Feb. The raid was completely successful. I foresaw Officer & 13 other ranks being made prisoners and a number of the enemy being killed, numerous our casualties were slight. The barrage was reported to be excellent. Complimentary telegrams from the Corps Commander were shown R Lt Col Paterson leading R.C.D. who attacked as well as detailed orders for the operation. Capt Tom Reed received from him personal reply or attached Fight Group. | Nancy |

Army Form C. 2118.

# WAR DIARY
## INTELLIGENCE SUMMARY
(Erase heading not required.)

| Place | Date | Hour | Summary of Events and Information | Remarks and references to Appendices |
|---|---|---|---|---|
| W. FENDRELEN | 17th | | To G.O.C. R.H.A. Second Right Group. | |
| | 18th | | Whit mule received that R.H. Gallagher & Staff reached dismt L/Col Harding's Staff 9th Bn Light Group H.Q. by 12 a.m. on 21st inst. V.I.R.H.A. relieving N.I.R.H.A. by 11 force date. | |
| | 19th | | Major E.M. James, Lieut D.I.O. R.H.A. returned from leave and reported encamped at N Battery R.H.A. The previous section of N.I.R.H.A. was relieved by a section of V.I.R.H.A. and withdrew to the wagon lines at TREFCON the remainder of the Battery withdrew from R.H.A. relieves by 11.0 a.m. 17th On R.H.A. and withdrew to its wagon lines at MONCHY LAGACHE | |
| MONCHY LAGACHE | 22nd | | L/Col W Harding D.O. R.H.A. discussed command of Cavalry Artillery brigade at ROUVROICOURT since L/Col P. Macullough L/t D.O. R.H.A. was probably on leave. On 17th Bn. new Billets at VINCHY LAGACHE N.I.R.H.A. at TREFCON 17th Brigade. Groups H.Q. at MONCHY LAGACHE. | |

Army Form C. 2118.

# WAR DIARY
*or*
# INTELLIGENCE SUMMARY.
*(Erase heading not required.)*

| Place | Date | Hour | Summary of Events and Information | Remarks and references to Appendices |
|---|---|---|---|---|
| | 26th | | H.Qrs. 17th Brigade R.H.A. and N Battery R.H.A. has been in action practically continuously from 20th to 28th November 1917 & the 21st February 1918. Capt. T.O.M. Bird joined H.Q. Cavalry Arty Corps to take up the duties of Reconnaissance Officer N/XVII R.H.A. Won 17th Brigade and 17th Bde Amm. Col were placed at the disposal of the 5th Cavalry Divn so enable same service church was sore 5th Cavalry Divn appears to be in absence of instructions for fight  in defensive sense in not available so to details the 17th Brigade R.H.A. is to accompany the divison as not | |

T.O.M. Bird
Captain R.H.A.
for R.H.A. Comm 17th Brigade R.H.A.

# WAR DIARY or INTELLIGENCE SUMMARY

Army Form C. 2118

295

1915 5th Div

Head Quarter
17th Bde... RHA

| Place | Date | Hour | Summary of Events and Information | Remarks and references to Appendices |
|---|---|---|---|---|
| BOUZINCOURT | MARCH | | From 1st March to 14th March R.Col visiting D10 R.H.A also as C.R.A Column. Armoured Artillery with Head Quarters at BOUZINCOURT. The Staff consisted of Major R Archer Houblon D.10. RHA acting Brigade Major. Major A.N. Harvard E.D.G. acting Staff Captain 1st – 3rd March. Capt T.A.H. Bond R.H.A. acting Staff Captain 4/3/21. Capt. K Carlisle R.F.A. acting Staff Captain 5th – 14th March. Reconnaissance made 4/3/21 Reconnaissances the RECON during N Battery R.H.A. were at wagon lines at Columns and Head Quarters at MENCHY LAGACHE. This period with the Columns and Head Quarters at MENCHY LAGACHE. The Artillery in the line consisted of Right Group commanded by R.Col. Elkins D16 RCHA {Left Group commanded by Lt Col T.E.B. Allenbyes D16 RHA | |

311th Army Tab Aty Brigade
D Battery R.H.A.
107th Battery 23rd AFA Brigade
C/23rd AFA Brigade

E + T Batteries RHA
A + B " RCHA
108th Battery 23rd AFA Bde
D/23rd AFA Brigade

# WAR DIARY
## INTELLIGENCE SUMMARY
*(Erase heading not required.)*

Army Form C. 2118.

| Place | Date | Hour | Summary of Events and Information | Remarks and references to Appendices |
|---|---|---|---|---|
| | March 3rd 1918 | | Capt T A H Bows adjutant 17th Regmt R.H.A. was appointed to the Brigade Hqrs Artillery Authority x 17th & N/RHA went in to Cavalry Corps Reserve | |
| | 9th 10/3/18 | | N/RHA went to support a raid on Cheese Tree and captured the enemy front line system between two points. 3 Prisoners were captured. | |
| | 14th | | Enr. no. aty. were relieved by 24th Armoured Artillery as the Cavalry being relieved in the line by the 24th Division. E Battery R.H.A. and a section of the B Brigade R.H.A Armd. Col. were transferred from the 3rd Cavalry Artillery to the 17th Bde R.H.A. The R.C.H.A. Brigade was transferred to the 3rd Cavalry Division with the Canadian Cavalry Brigade. G & N Batteries became Batteries in Anti-Tank Reserve | |
| MONCHY LABACHE | 15th | | G. on the 11th Aus front N. gun the 24th Div front. G/1RHA moved to HAMELET from its bivouac behind VRAIGNES after being relieved in the line. N/RHA moved from TREFCON to VRAIGNES Hqrs & Column Presumed at MONCHY LAGACHE | |

# WAR DIARY or INTELLIGENCE SUMMARY

Army Form C. 2118.

| Place | Date | Hour | Summary of Events and Information | Remarks and references to Appendices |
|---|---|---|---|---|
| MONCHY LAGACHE | March 16th/17th | | Col Bolton & the adjutant visited 5th Cav Bde HQ at PONTRU-METZ. Major R.H. Elliott was posted to command E Battery RHA vice Major H Young. Minutes | |
| | 18th | | News received from Cavalry Corps that the Regiment would not accompany the 5th Cavalry Division to EGYPT. | |
| | 20th | | W.O.C. enquiries. Cpt HK Raines MC RHA RHQ to command 42nd DAC. Capt Howman RFA was appointed to command the battery in his place | |
| | 21st | | German attack opened about 4.30 am by a very heavy bombardment. No news received to noon. Orders were sent to 16th Bde HQ where Retirees in the morning and sent orders to I & N at about noon. E Battery were ordered to retire by Jul to MAHELET. West on to 24th Bde HQ and found N Battery had also been ordered to retire near VERMAND CEMETARY. It appears that the enemy was by a Rsk | |

# WAR DIARY
## INTELLIGENCE SUMMARY.
(Erase heading not required.)

Army Form C. 2118.

| Place | Date | Hour | Summary of Events and Information | Remarks and references to Appendices |
|---|---|---|---|---|
| | March 22nd | | met and a very heavy bombardment his attacks in great force & rushed our outpost line before we had time to retake the infantry attack his began LE VERGUIER and ESSIGNY reamed held out well, but it appears that the enemy got this 10 no line in places. His views on attacks were received by the 11 Q. MONCHY LAGACHE was found in the enemy 20/21 and withdrew by a H.Q. gun in the early morning a. H. Connel went to the G Battery adjutant went to the N Battery Forward army heavy fighting going on & our infantry but as the queries were 60th Div up to support 24th Div MONCHY LAGACHE shelling agreed to the afternoon. No orders received from XIXth Corps but it was decided to move the brigade & head Quarters back to ENNEMAIN.  March at about 5 p.m. | |

Army Form C. 2118.

# WAR DIARY
## INTELLIGENCE SUMMARY.
*(Erase heading not required.)*

Instructions regarding War Diaries and Intelligence Summaries are contained in F. S. Regs., Part II. and the Staff Manual respectively. Title pages will be prepared in manuscript.

| Place | Date | Hour | Summary of Events and Information | Remarks and references to Appendices |
|---|---|---|---|---|
| ENNEMAIN | March 23rd 1918 | | After reveille this a.m. of the Brigade of the 1st Div Arty on ENNEMAIN that all vehicles were to cross the SOMME | |
| | | 7 am | Marches to MISERY arriving about 5 am. Roads very bad. | |
| | | 8 am | Went to VILLER CARBONNEL to the XIX Corps HQ, were unable to obtain orders. Found N Battery in VILLER CARBONNEL with orders to march MORCHAIN to defend the river crossing. Here Capt Chapman asst G/HHA was wounded and missing. Lt Col Sterling was also by a Genl Mare-Marie to act as CRA 24th D.A. Group while to General incapacitated. The remainder of the artillery of the 24th, 50th and 8th Divisions were | |
| | | 3 pm | above. HQ moved to CHAULNES | |
| | | 4 pm | Established near the 58 D Prisoner of War log Camp Here enemy had crossed the river to rev. of SARGNY 24th D.A. consisted of 10th & 107th Brigades R.F.A. (2 batteries each) 311th AFA Brigade 23rd AFA Brigade N. I Batteries RHA | |

# WAR DIARY
## or
## INTELLIGENCE SUMMARY.

Army Form C. 2118.

(Erase heading not required.)

| Place | Date | Hour | Summary of Events and Information | Remarks and references to Appendices |
|---|---|---|---|---|
| CHAULNES | 24th | | A. & B. Batteries R.H.A. 25th Brigade R.F.A. and 6th Bde. R.F.A. Battery R.F.A. night spent at CHAULNES. Heavy fighting all day with the enemy strung across the river between PARENT and EPANÉCOURT. Not every day are infantry getting worn out with four days incessant fighting and marching all accounts shew that the gunners fought with great determination and had many excellent targets - often over the open sights. Enemy casualties must be very heavy, but he is employing masses of troops & the sheer weight of his troops tells against his two weak fresh troops throughout was very heavy, but up to infanteers to my knowledge have been to keep, but have retreated frequently that the twice tho after the first movement for any but his field, in was closed up, and as ruled by any regular retirement covered unceasingly by the great fire No ce. | |

Army Form C. 2118.

# WAR DIARY or INTELLIGENCE SUMMARY.
(Erase heading not required.)

| Place | Date | Hour | Summary of Events and Information | Remarks and references to Appendices |
|---|---|---|---|---|
| CHARMES | March 25th | | Capt. TAM Ross R.H.A. took over the duties of acting Staff Captain i/c R.D.A. chiefly concerning the supply of ammunition which was very difficult to cope with. Five under enemy shell fire continued. Head Quarters withdrew to LIHAN in the afternoon, the Colonels having gone on to CAIX the previous afternoon. | |
| ROUVREY EN MITERIE | 5 pm | | late in the evening, H.Q. withdrew to ROGERS EN SANTERRE. A very critical anxious day as our troops were worn out & the enemy still attacking in great force and over flanks were at one time in the air. N Battery in action near PRELY near Lt. T.E. Beevor R.H.A. who commanded G Battery after Champion's loss has been killed. He was only distinguished himself by pushing the battery with great dash & gallantry had E.A M°THERS of N. Battery wounded to for rather to far rather rather suffered as regards at any rate have been reported and high appear to have distressed the Pressers have been tuned the high reputation & tradition of the Horse Artillery | |

# WAR DIARY
## INTELLIGENCE SUMMARY

Army Form C. 2118.

| Place | Date | Hour | Summary of Events and Information | Remarks and references to Appendices |
|-------|------|------|-----------------------------------|--------------------------------------|
| | March 26 | | Ron Hicks - Nurse nursed wounded of 24th D.B. Col Harkey remaining to assist him. Lt Tutton & Sergt Goodnight with the light horses of the Ammunition Column attached to E Battery thence to BEAUCOURT | |
| DEMUIN | | | HO this night at DEMUIN. Situation still very critical. Everyone tried out. Capt Bushby & HQ personnel at usual interesting and encouraging cheerful Rev. Daughty Turner Craig and Gn. Sykes, did useful work as other ket. Lt N.S. Command Battery of HQ Head Quarters. — was key of 24th D.B. as P.O. | |
| DEMUIN | 27th | | Scheme moved to COTTENCHY late in the morning. HO remained at DEMUIN | |
| | 28th | | HQ moves to ONTREL. weather turned cold wet French re inforcements came up but Enemy still advanced Head Major Elliot has assumed command of E Battery & Bat- | |

# WAR DIARY
## INTELLIGENCE SUMMARY

Army Form C. 2118.

| Place | Date | Hour | Summary of Events and Information | Remarks and references to Appendices |
|---|---|---|---|---|
| | March | | | |
| CASTEL to COTTENCHY | 29th March 1918 | | 2nd Hussars of E/RHA had been killed. Headquarters moved to COTTENCHY. Assumed HQ commanding at CASTEL between at COTTENCHY. N Battery in action near DEMUIN and E/ just north of there. Enemy's advance appears to have been hurried up but fighting is still very heavy and before the advance the Cavalry in action. Almost in to open warfare in her developed. | |
| DOMART BOVES | 30th | | HQ moved again to DOMART were to have stopped but to BOVES at ingest at the 2nd D/A were supporting the 20th Div. Heavy fighting all day with the result that our line was held. Major E.M. Spiers 4th D/10 R.H.A and Capt F.D. Fenton R.H.A had both been wounded. N/Battery & Trained M.C. R.H.A. was commanded N. Battery Lt CAMMELL R.H.A went | |
| OTTENCHY | 31st | | moved back to COTTENCHY to form N. Battery. To receive enemy up to face in the last 3 days during the advanced very little | |

EAGLE TROOP    RHA

21/29.    3    18
_____

## NOTES

on the part taken by the EAGLE TROOP R.H.A.
in the fighting from March 21st to 29th inclusive.

---

**VRAIGNES.**
**Thursday**
**March 21st.**

The Battery in wagon lines as Mobile Anti-Tank Reserve. Prepared to move at short notice to engage enemy tanks from prepared positions. (See Anti Tank Scheme, Map)

**4:30 a.m.**

Wakened at 4:30 a.m. by heavy and continuous bombardment on the whole front. "Stand to" ordered and horses fed. All had breakfast as soon as ready. Weather very foggy. Orders received from 19th Corps through 24th D.A. to be ready to move forward at 20 minutes' notice.

**11:0 a.m.**

Weather cleared. Other battery wagon lines in VRAIGNES sending up ammunition and Orderlies to and fro. News filtering through. Bosch apparently placed heavy barrage on all batteries and also on places well in rear. Last hour gas. Infantry attack commenced 8:30 a.m.. At this time enemy attacking main line ("Red Line") which ran SE from VERGUIER. (See Map) TREFCON and CAULAINCOURT heavily shelled, also HANCOURT; trying for dump on HANCOURT-VRAIGNES road probably. Danger of tanks being past, horses were harnessed, but not saddled up. Dimmers up 12:0 noon. Officers lunched at the same time. Lt. Steevens of 'C' R.H.A. said that JEANCOURT and Valley was full of gas, also VENDELLES, and railway cutting. Lt. Patrick of 'C' wounded.

**1:30 p.m.**

Orders received from 19th Corps that 'N' placed under 24th D.A. and to move at once to a position in neighbourhood of Vermand Cemetery, but "to reconnoitre carefully as Bosch might be there already". Moved at once and in action by 2:0 p.m..

(N.B. The seriousness of the situation was not yet appreciated, but it was believed generally that the Bosch would be stopped and driven back, and consequently preparations were made for a night out only, not a wholesale evacuation and retirement. Orders were issued to wagon line assuming horses would return there as in stationary warfare.

**VERMAND.**
**2:0 p.m.**

Four guns were placed in action North of the Cemetery two guns in a field west of it, one of them being in an empty stable. O.P. on a high embankment about ½ mile E in centre of VERMAND. Liaison here with the Infantry. Shelled MAISSEMY and ground to south of OMIGNON.

'I' Battery R.H.A. came into action on our right flank. 'A' and 'B' batteries R.C.H.A. which had retired from positions near VENDELLES also came into action near us on our left.

Situation very uncertain. Enemy in great numbers. Our Infantry putting up strong resistance in VADENCOURT but the enemy seemed to be getting on south of the river. Lt. Smith went forward to reconnoitre and was fired on by M.G's from south bank of the river when in vicinity of BIHEUCOURT ("Brown Line") which ran East of railway.

railway East of VENDELLES S.E. to River OMIGNON at BIHEUCOURT. (See Map)

Firing Battery teams forming "Advanced Wagon Line" remained ¼ mile in rear of guns. Word sent to B.S.M. Farlie D.C.M. at VRAIGNES of this new arrangement. Information regarding the situation sent to Colonel Stirling at MONCHY LAGACHE.

Battery in Right Group 24th D.A. under Lt. Col. Spiller D.S.O.. Headquarters at SAILOR WOOD near POEUILLY.

Rations, forage and horse rugs sent up. Gun limbers remained up close all night, but F.B.W. teams and detachment horses moved about 800 yds further back to a more comfortable and sheltered spot for the night. These teams were off-saddled. The night passed off quietly.

| | |
|---|---|
| VERMAND.<br>Friday<br>March 22nd. | Thick fog again covered everything. The Bosch attacked the "Red Line" heavily on the whole front. VADENCOURT was taken by 10:30 a.m.. LE VERGUIER fell about 11:0 a.m.<br>Limbers moved up closer to the guns.<br>Out of touch with Lt. Col. Spiller.<br>The enemy reached VILLECHOLES forcing the "West Kents" north of the river to retire. Our Infantry had lost very heavily.<br>After consulting with Lt. Col. Anderson, Hussars, commanding the tropps in VERMAND, the C.O. withdrew the battery some 1000 yards to a position on the crest west of VERMAND.<br>While on the cemetery position the battery was attacked by two enemy formations of 15 aeroplanes flying at from 500 feet to 1000 ft; these were driven off with rifle and Lewis Gun fire - Bdr. Dobbs - Several salvos fell in and round the battery during the withdrawal, but there were no casualties.<br>The Light Xn. A.C. joined the Advanced Wagon Line here.<br>Warning sent to B.S.M.Farlie, D.C.M. to pack up as much as possible, and be prepared to move. He packed everything, and the only loss was three casks of beer from the canteen which were emptied out. |
| VERMAND.<br>1000 yds west<br>of -<br>1:0 p.m. | From the new position engaged targets on both banks of the river near VADENCOURT with four guns. The remaining Xn. in action at right angles to battery, shelled enemy masses on slopes of BOIS de HOLNON, south of river. |
| 3:0 p.m. | Enemy penetrated into VERMAND, and our infantry being driven out, retired through the guns, and on through the "Green Line" which ran roughly North, and South just East of villages BERNES, FLECHIN, POEUILLY, CAULAINCOURT to BEAUVOIS. (See Map) The 50th Division were digging in there. The battery then withdrew through CAULAINCOURT and TERTRY to a position in the R.E. stables at TREFCON. |
| R.E.Stables<br>TREFCON<br>½ m.N.W.of - | Lt. Towell went forward to our old huts in TREFCON to observe, and established touch with the Infantry in the "Green Line". |
| 4:0 p.m. | B.S.M.Farlie D.C.M.forced to evacuate VRAIGNES,and retired to MONS-EN-CHAUSSEE.<br>Enemy massing in VILLEVEQUE and preparing for assault on "Green Line", were shelled with effect.<br>Lt./ |

Lt. Mitchell sent to get touch with Group H.Q. Several batteries could be seen in action in the valley east of TERTRY N. bank of river, and there he found Lt. Col. Elkins D.S.O., R.C.H.A..

Lt. Mitchell returned with orders from Lt.Col.Elkins that the battery was now in his group, and was to retire to a position about one mile south of MONS-EN-CHAUSSEE. (Trefcon!)

While in this position, a battery of 8" Howitzers with caterpillars was withdrawn from SAVY while Infantry held up the Bosch on the east edge of village within 300 yds. A very good show.

6:0 p.m.

The enemy made a successful assault on the "Green Line" at 6:0 p.m. Friday evening. Lt. Towell did not leave the O.P. till the "Green Line" was taken and enemy infantry nearly in TREFCON.

Marched at 6:30 p.m. via MONCHY LAGACHE to position 1500 yards south of MONS-EN-CHAUSSEE which was reached safely just before dark. Took route through MONCHY LAGACHE as enemy were shelling the bridge over OMIGNON at TERTRY behind us very heavily.

'G' Battery (the other battery of our Brigade) had till now been attached to 66th Division. D.R. arrived with letter from Capt. J.A.M.Bond, Adjt. 17th Brigade R.H.A. saying that Lt. Col. W. Stirling D.S.O. commanding the brigade hoped to collect his two batteries at VILLERS CARBONNELL the following day.

MONS-EN-
CHAUSSEE.
Friday
22nd March.

Brigade H.Q. and Main Column located at VILLERS CARBONNELL for night, having evacuated MONCHY LAGACHE during the afternoon when it was heavily shelled.

C.O. reported personally to Group Commander in MONS at mid-night with this letter, and obtained permission to march to VILLERS CARBONNELL forthwith.

Saturday
23rd March
2:0 a.m.

Started at 2:0 a.m.. Battery marched via Athies, ST. CHRIST.

Rear wagon line and Light Xn. A.C. via BRIE under orders of Captain.

VILLERS
CARBONNELL.
8:0 a.m.

The Captain's party on arrival found battery already there. Placed again under 24th D.A. and ordered to proceed south at once to MORCHAIN. Battery had arrived 7:0 a.m. and had already watered, fed, and breakfasted, and moved at once.

Captain's party watered, fed, and breakfasted, and then followed on.

Before leaving, visited 19th Corps H.Q. in VILLERS CARBONNELL; just moving and got latest news, and some maps.

Saw Brig. Gen. Hoare Nairne C.B.,C.M.G., commanding 24th D.A. he said 8th Division were coming up, and attempt was to be made to hold up Bosch on line of Somme. He is now commanding all army brigades in 19th Corps. Col. Stirling is acting C.R.A. 24th D.A..

Got some maps. Also saw Lt. Johns of Cavalry Corps, Signal Squadron, and obtained some extra telephone wire which came in very useful.

MORCHAIN.

Met Major Archer-Houblon D.S.O. commanding 'I' Battery/

Battery R.H.A., Four guns put in action east of the town on left of 'I' R.H.A., and two kept in reserve. (Rt.Xn. Lt. Lloyd.)

Lt. Mitchell went forward to find O.P. and get in touch with Infantry.

About 11:0 a.m.
1st. Cavalry Division arrived, and one brigade crossed the Somme to east bank.

Saw Lt. Col. W.E. Clarke commanding R.H.A. 1st Cavalry Division. Covering crossings at PARGNY and BETHENCOURT.

Attacked by aeroplanes. Village shelled. Moved wagon lines, but followed by aeroplane which put artillery on to us again.

Split up teams and continued to dodge about till we retired. Plane never let us alone. Dr. Gomm wounded, and seven or eight horses killed.

Battery fired a very large number of rounds and had some very good targets east of Somme.

Portion of Infantry 8th Division arrived in the afternoon, and moved up to the Somme under very heavy fire, suffering severe losses.

March 23rd/24th.
During the night the Bosch forced the crossings of the Somme, driving in the cavalry screen. 8th Hussars lost heavily.

March 24th. Sunday.
Infantry retired to crest line just east of MORCHAIN. Remnants of a battalion of the Worcestershire Regiment, 8th Division, 25th. Infantry Brigade - Staff Capt. Burney -.

Battery forced to conform to the general retirement.

Lt. Lloyd took his section into action south of the main road to PERTAIN, and about 1000 yds west of MORCHAIN O.P. in an apple tree.

Excellent shooting on the Bosch crossing the open.

Captain Fenton ordered Rear Wagon Line to retire to a position west of OMIECOURT from PERTAIN where they had spent the night 23rd/24th.

PERTAIN.
1:30 p.m.
Captain Fenton then selected a position for the remaining four guns in west edge of PERTAIN, and left them in charge of Lt. Towell and went forward to report to C.O. who had remained with Lt. Lloyd.

2:0 p.m.
Infantry commenced retirement to wired line west of MORCHAIN.

Lt. Towell received orders from Capt. Hughes, R.C.H.A Adjt. "Elkins Group", to "Take the 4 guns under his command into action in the open with as little dead ground as possible to engage the enemy crossing the crest north of MORCHAIN". An order was also received from G.O.C., R.A., V Army, ordering guns to fight to last etc., as Bosch "must be stopped".

Captain Fenton returned at the moment this was taking place and ordered "stand fast". Guns were put under cover of village in readiness, and position to be occupied should the need arise, selected. It did not. One horse killed.

4:0 p.m.
A further withdrawal took place, and four guns went into action on the eastern outskirts, of OMIECOURT. Here we had 'I' on our right, 'A' and 'B' R.C.H.A., and an 18pdr. battery on our left.

All batteries had run out of Ammunition except ourselves, and we gave each one wagon load.

Lt. Lloyd's Xn. retired at dusk, and went into reserve with the Rear Wagon Line.

The night passed quietly.

| | |
|---|---|
| OMIECOURT.<br>Monday,<br>25th March.<br>11:0 a.m. | Lt. Mitchell, on liaison in PERTAIN, wounded and evacuated.<br>"40,000 Germans" reported advancing on DRESLINCOURT slightly to our right front.<br>Some enemy machine gunners got between the O.P. and and battery, and Lt. Towell had to gallop to get away.<br>12:0 noon - Orders received to retire by batteries from the left. Battery and advanced Wagon Line came under shrapnel fire here in the open. Infantry falling back on OMIECOURT.<br>'I' and ourselves moved south of the village on a previously reconnoitred track, as village was being heavily shelled, a possibility that had been foreseen. Those batteries which retired through the village, suffered casualties.<br>German Spy dressed as a Staff Captain caused a panic here amongst infantry transport by raising cry of "the German Cavalry are through; save yourselves".<br>Rear Wagon Line ordered to retire to a position west of LIHONS on road to ROSIERES.<br>Battery had some splendid shooting before retiring. |
| CHAULNES.<br>Railway<br>Station.1 p.m. | Occupied excellent position selected by C.O.. Found valuable loot of forage and food; Good water. |
| 4:0 p.m. | Situation now very obscure, and infantry again falling back. Country "crawling" with Bosch.<br>Our spare rifles commandeered to arm stray details. One platoon in trenches east of CHAULNES consisted of Tank Corps Personnel officered by R.F.C.. |
| 4:30 p.m.<br><br>LIHONS<br>6:30 p.m. | Retired again, and took up a very awkward position with 'I' on the high ground west of CHAULNES. Good shooting. No sooner in action, than we retired again to position with 'I' in a field west of LIHONS where we spent the night. Very cold.<br>Rear Wagon Line to ROSIERES. Batteries of 8th Division in action near us. |
| Tuesday,<br>26th March. | Enemy round right flank, and Ordered to retire through ROSIERES and find a position to cover VRELY. Position south of CAIX selected by Captain Fenton. Rear Wagon Line to position west of village.<br>All six guns in action by 12:35 p.m. in new position Rear Wagon Line shelled and two men wounded. Moved slightly. Lt. Towell on liaison, then Lt. Smith. Quiet night. |
| Wednesday<br>27th March. | 12:0 Noon. Advanced 1500 yds to get better targets. Spent the night here. |
| Thursday,<br>28th March.<br>500 yds East of<br>Wood on CAIX-<br>LE QUESNEL<br>Road. | Bosch came on, and we retired again about 8:30 a.m. to an excellent position about 2000 yds. back.<br>Bosch shelled north end of wood heavily, and we were also attacked again by a formation of 15 aeroplanes flying low. These we drove off. No. 6. gun run forward to open position to engage enemy attacking LE QUESNEL on our right flank. Excellent shooting with remaining guns on VRELY at 2500 yds. Rear Wagon Line to BEAUCOURT Withdrew again about mid-day to a new position near BEAUCOURT. |

Copse 1½ miles N.E. BEAUCOURT.

Retirement carried out by sections under shell fire. Enemy in LE QUESNEL. Believed ourselves surrounded. Saw Lt.Col.Allardyce D.S.O. 6?R.H.A. 4th Cavalry Division, who considered situation very serious. Met French reinforcements here.

Near MAISON BLANCHE.
3:30 p.m.

Retired again 3:30 p.m. to position near MAISON BLANCHE, but ordered to move N. to DEMUIN.

DEMUIN.
28th March.

Came into action just south of the village about 7:0 p.m. Pitch dark and raining. Spent night here. Plenty of food and forage.

C.O. accompanied by Captain Fenton reported to Group H.Q. located in the village, and there saw Brig. Gen. Hunter 61st Division, commanding the troops in DEMUIN. Subaltern of 'I' R.H.A. reports that French Troops, who had relieved our Infantry, and whom we were covering, had retired leaving no one in the line. (Lt. Eastman).

11:0 p.m.

Group Commander then ordered all batteries to send out a mounted patrol to ascertain truth of this report, and clear up situation. Lt. Smith took out our patrol. All made same report - "No French" - and all had been on till they had located Bosch by contact.

Battery Lewis guns taken up into trench line under a Subaltern, and remained there all night. Report sent back, and finally French, who had retired through a mistaken order, returned between 4:0 and 5:0 a.m..
Saw 'H' Battery R.H.A. and also 16th Brigade R.H.A 'A' 'Q' and 'U' here.

Friday
29th March.

Bosch shelled DEMUIN heavily early in morning.
No casualties.
Rear Wagon Line was now at DOMART.

1 Mile S.E.
of THENNES.

Retired from DEMUIN 10:0 a.m. to a new position on forward slope near THENNES, where we stopped all day.
Firing in the neighbourhood of MAISON BLANCHE.
Dr. Hankin, R. wounded.

5:0 p.m.

Moved further south to a position near wood of VILLERS AUX ERABLES. 'I' R.H.A. on the reverse slope to our left rear. R.C.H.A batteries on our left with a French "75" battery in between.
Rear Wagon Line at HAILLES, and later west of CASTEL.
in/

7:0 p.m.

When the O.P. Major G.M.Spencer Smith and Captain Fenton were wounded by the same bullet. Shortly after the battery retired across the river, and they were taken to the dressing station at CASTEL, and eventually reached ROUEN from which place they went to England, and were struck off the strength.

Lt. Towell took command, and commanded the battery till April 6th, when it was withdrawn from action, and the new C.O. joined - Major C.W.Massey D.S.O., M.C., R.H.A., -

Saturday 30 March.

The battery recrossed to the EAST bank of R. AVRE & came into action near THENNES.

30th March.   The battery had four men killed, and some wounded. Bad luck, but on the whole we had been as usual wonderfully lucky, and had very few casualties.

THE RETIREMENT WAS NOW AT AN END.

Gratifying letters were received from Brig. Gen. Sandys C.M.G., R.A., Commanding Artillery, 19th Corps, and from Brig. Gen. Hoare Nairne, C.B., C.M.G., R.A. C.R.A., of 24th Division with regard to the part played by the battery in the retirement, and no less than ten Military Medals were given, and two M.C's.

The example set by batteries R.H.A. was said to havebeen magnificent.

'G' R.H.A. our sister troop, suffered severely. They were commanded throughout the retirement by a subaltern. Captain Chapman had been wounded and been wounded and taken prisoner on March 22nd, in ROISEL when trying to rally the retiring infantry. In addition to the loss of this officer, Lieuts. Beever and Hindle were killed.

The officers of the EAGLE TROOP at this time were -

Commanding          Major G.M. Spencer Smith, D.S.O., R.H.A.,
2nd. in cmd.        Captain G.A. Fenton, R.H.A.,
                    Lieut. G.W. Towell, M.C., R.H.A.,
                    Lieut. R.L. Lloyd, R.H.A.,
                    Lieut. E.A. Mitchell, R.H.A.,
                    Lieut. V.B. Cammell, R.H.A.,

Attached.           2/Lieut. J.B.H. Smith, R.F.A..

Lieut. Cammell was however detached with Brigade Headquarters throughout these operations.

The following received Decorations:

Bar to M.C.         Lieut. Towell.
M.C.                Lieut. Lloyd.

Bar to M.M.         Sgt. Barnes.
                    Cpl. Oakley.

M.M.                Sgt. Murfitt.
                    Sgt. Stubbs.
                    Sgt. Kalmer.
                    Bdr. Hovells.
                    Gnr. Davis.
                     "  Groves.
                     "  Mulholland.
                     "  Stenson.

The battery was already in possession of -

1 D.S.O.
1 M.C.
1 M.V.O.
2 D.C.M's.
1 M.M. and bar.
4 M.M's.
2 Long Service.
84 Mons Stars.

besides several War Medals for service in South Africa, Egypt, and India.

In addition, two Foreign Decorations had been awarded to men of the Troop, viz: -

1 Belgian Croix de Guerre.
1 Belgian Military Medal.

Decorations won with the troop by Officers and men who have since left it are -

1 D.S.O.
2 M.C's.
3 D.C.M's.
1 M.M.

Major Massey who took over command vice Major Spencer Smith, has the D.S.O. and M.C., He has since been wounded and succeeded by Major C.I. McKay, who has the M.C..

Numerous decorations and rewards for service have been won by officers and men of the troop since leaving it on promotion, commission, or through wounds.

The officers' casualties during the retreat were -

Major G.M. Spencer Smith, D.S.O.  )
Captain G.A. Fenton               )  Wounded.
Lieut. E.A. Mitchell              )

In addition four men were killed, and eight wounded.

Lieut. Towell became Captain vice Captain Fenton, and Lieut. Lloyd became Captain of 'G' R.H.A. vice Captain Chapman.

*Captain Towell was killed while temporarily in command of the battery on August 8th & was a very great loss. He combined the very highest qualities of courage & ability with a personality which inspired confidence in all he came in contact with. He was the most reliable officer we had, possessed of sound judgement and always cool & collected in a crisis.*

## LESSONS which may be learnt from the RETREAT.

(With general notes and comments.)

1. ### INITIAL EFFICIENCY.

    The R.H.A. batteries had an enormous advantage in having been compelled to keep up training in mobile warfare. They had not, at any rate recently, suffered many casualties, and their personnel was probably better trained for moving warfare than that of batteries R.F.A.

    Battery staffs were probably better equipped and more accustomed to altering positions rapidly, their equipment being specially arranged for M.W., and in good state.

2. ### GAS.

    It was noticeable that, after the preliminary bombardment, few gas shells were experienced; there is therefore less chance of getting them in M.W., due no doubt to the very careful way in which they have to be transported.

3. ### INFORMATION and LIAISON.

    Great difficulty was experienced throughout in keeping up good liaison with our infantry, the result being that information was not properly circulated, and everyone was constantly in the dark as to the progress of events on either flank, as well as to the front.

    On one occasion at least - on March 26th - the Staff imagined the infantry to be holding a line considerably further west than was the case, and battery positions chosen to cover this line were very much too far back. The error was discovered by our liaison officer, and information as to the correct position of our infantry was circulated. The batteries all had to move forward.

    It must be remembered that our infantry were in many cases greatly disorganized before they started to retire, having been very severely handled by the enemy. They were therefore not in a fit state either as regards organization or equipment, to commence a long and arduous retreat.

    Our experience was that our infantry were insufficiently supplied with such stores as Very Lights, Flares, etc:. They had nothing to mark the positions they were holding, while the Hun was continually marking his advance by little white flares.

    Too much importance cannot be laid on the necessity for circulating all information promptly.

    There is little doubt that the general lack of information and the prevalence of German Spies, led to unnecessary retirements on the part of our infantry on more than one occasion.

    Once a real panic was very narrowly averted. It was started - it was said - by a man in the uniform of a British Staff Captain who shouted to everyone to save themselves as the German Cavalry were on them.
    This happened at OMIECOURT on March 25th.

On more than one occasion it was necessary to send out mounted patrols in the evening to find out -
    (a) The dispositions of our forces,
    (b) The positions held by the Hun.

As an instance - officers' patrols were sent out by all batteries on the evening of March 28th., and all returned with the same report:- viz. - that there were no troops in front of us, although French troops were expected, and giving us the position of the German patrols.

The Lewis guns of the 4 batteries, with their gunners were then sent forward under a subaltern, and the gap held by them till morning.

Subaltern officers rendered really useful service on these patrols, and displayed great dash in their execution

The liaison with the French at this time appeared to be very unsatisfactory - between formations, that is.

Throughout, we had 1 subaltern detached, with orderlies, solely for liaison purposes, and were generally well and quickly informed regarding changes or impending changes in the situation.

## LUCAS LAMPS.

The Lucas Daylight Lamp proved of immense value. At least 4 per battery should be the authorized establishment. Spare cells, bulbs, etc., for all electrical equipment in LARGE NUMBERS are essential.

In these, as in all signal stores, we had very much more than our authorized establishment.

## 5. TEAMS.

Teams to remove all vehicles in the gun line must be kept at the gun position, or as near as possible.

There appears to be no possible alternative to this, although it is admitted that it is throwing a great strain on men and horses, as harness can never be removed for long, if at all, and certainly never at night.

Is this really very hard? Is it not what would have been expected, and regarded as "normal" before this War?

Again in connection with Wagon Lines, the idea of an advanced wagon line, as small as possible, is only normal. F.A.T. puts the Wagon Line close to the position, generally to the rear, and slightly to the flank.

It seems that the very "Special Methods" which have been produced by the unexpected development of trench warfare, make any return to the normal appear a venture into the abnormal.

This applies also to certain reference to points of Drill (see para: 15, "withdrawing of rounds preparatory to a retirement.")

It is also of paramount importance to improve, and mark all exits to positions, to enable a move to be easily undertaken at night.

It was noticeable that the Germans never seemed to attempt a serious move during darkness, preferring to come forward at dawn.

## 6. SHOEING – WATERING – FEEDING – RUGGING UP – OFF-SADDLING.

Horses were fed four times a day. Watered, whenever possible, and we got water at least twice a day except on one occasion. A team or two teams at a time only.

Horse-rugs. Each horse carried its own rug round its neck, and it was opened and spread out at any long halt.

Now, as regards the other points, let it be clear first of all that we had an "Advanced Wagon Line" consisting of Firing Battery Limbers and teams, and detachment horses only, and a "Rear Wagon Line" consisting of the First Line Wagons, transport Wagons and the Light Xn. Ammunition Column.

The Rear Wagon Line was always able to off-saddle and rest horses, and also generally managed to water three or four times a day. Consequently all that was necessary as regards shoeing etc. was to see that each team had its turn in the Rear Wagon Line, which was in itself easily accomplished in the normal method of ammunition supply. (The latter is dealt with elsewhere.)

## 7. GUN-TEAMS.

In order that these horses should also have a chance of being off-saddled, and looked over properly, we used to change round Gun – F.B.W. and F.L.W. teams at suitable intervals, generally every third day. Impossible to lay down any hard and fast rule. Individual horses and teams had to be considered.

Two nose-bags a horse. Those for hand horses of teams on limber footboards.

## 8. HARNESS FITTING.

All the harness had been fitted so carefully long before and constant attention paid to it, that there were practically no galls. Sore backs too were avoided, in spite of the length of time horses remained saddled up, by careful attention, and good hand-rubbing whenever saddles could be removed.

## 9. FORAGE.

Unless the situation was quiet, hay was for the most part consumed always in Rear Wagon Line, when we got any. A bale would be got up for the advanced teams, but there was always a risk of waste.

The corn ration was supplemented by a large amount which we were able to loot and carry with us from CHAULNES and DEMUIN. Horses must have had from 16 to 20 lbs a day at least. There was always a surplus at the ration dumps too which we invariably secured. Sgt. Martin D.C.M., M.M., (and bar.)

Chaff cut in Rear Wagon Line and sent up in sacks.
We got a lot of abandoned linseed cake.

To the plentitude of corn, the horse rugs (which were invaluable on cold nights), and the even division of labour and in spite of the reduction in their watering, must be attributed the excellent condition of the horses, which stood the test well. Only a few of the more 'difficult' horses fell away at all, while the 'good doers' did even better. Orderlies' horses had the hardest time, but were changed from time to time.

Two shoeing smiths only with the "Firing Battery". The Farrier, and four shoeing smiths with Rear Wagon Line. Farrier did excellent work, and deserves a great deal of credit. - Farrier, Q.M.S. Chinery, D.C.M. -

10.
As regards the drawing of rations and forage, this was Sergeant Martin's department.

11.
In the Rear Wagon Line, the Sgt. Major commanded, Q.M.S. attended to ammunition and stores, Farrier to the horses, and the Asst. B.Q.M.S. - Sgt. Martin - to the rations and forage.

12. RATIONS.

We generally retired at 9:0 a.m. and 3:0 p.m. about. As soon as the evening retirement was over, and we had occupied a position for the night, Sgt. Martin left with two G.S.Wagons for the ration dump. He often had to do 10 miles there, and 10 miles back. On his return, the rations would be divided up for Rear Wagon Line, Advanced Wagon Line, Gun Line, Officers Mess, and distributed accordingly. On occasions it was necessary further to subdivide matters when there was a detached section.

Cooks were on occasions foolish, for should a move occur they had to carry their dixies on the Wagons. If they did not keep their eyes open, the wagons might then go off leaving them with no food. This happened once; and on other occasions they were not very sensible. Once they threw away the men's tea when a move was ordered, although it was only 500 to 600 yards, and they could easily have carried it.

13. OFFICERS' MESS.

Officers' Mess food was invariably cooked in the Rear Wagon Line by Gunner Cox, and brought up by Bdr. Rossiter, the Mess butler, mounted. He never failed to appear at the right moment.

Rations were good throughout.

The food question was all important as we got very little sleep.

There was plenty of opportunity for securing milk, and chickens etc. en route. At DEMUIN we killed, and ate a pig.

-13-

**14. QUARTERMASTERS STORES.**

The battery started well equipped in everything, and our only need during the fighting was to replenish our reserve of buffer oil which we did via the Main Ammunition Column.

N.k. - Regarding the greatly increased use of electric equipment of all sorts -

Would it be possible, in prolonged operations in open warfare such as occurred in March, to keep the Army supplied with the necessary refills, spares, etc?

Surely anyhow, since stores have been so vastly increased transport should be adequately increased also?

**15. AMMUNITION SUPPLY.**

This worked smoothly, and well throughout. Considerable resource was shown by the Junior N.C.O's taking wagons to replenish.

The general rule was that the firing battery wagons were at the advanced wagon line, and the first line, and light Xn A.C. were at the rear wagon line.

When more ammunition was needed, the first line would come up, the firing battery go back, and fill from the light Xn. and remain in rear wagon line while the lightXn. would then go and fill up from the Main Column, and return to rear wagon line. In other words, "normal ammunition supply". We always had a line of wagons full in the rear wagon line in this way, except once, when after heavy firing, the light Xn. had not yet returned from filling up, and the need being urgent, we sent our wagons straight back to the Main Column. March 27th.)

Whenever a section was in reserve, its wagons were preserved full, and the Xn. was self contained and intact.

On several occasions when a retirement was imminent, the wagons were emptied and the rounds placed by the guns. This after all, is only Drill as laid down in F.A.T. B.Q.M.S. Brundish did very good work superintending matters in the Rear Wagon Line.

**16. DRILL.**

The ordinary drill for a retirement - i.e. Captain to select new position - was not always adhered to; it depended very much on the circumstances.

**17. TRANSPORT.**

We had more than our authorised transport, and could not have achieved what we did without it. The inadequacy of the present establishment under present conditions has often been pointed out, and was borne out by the fact that the majority of batteries lost all their stores. We lost nothing.

When both battery and ration dump are continually moving back, if one has to dump one's stores to go and fetch supplies, it must eventually end in their abandonment.

With our system of having separate vehicles for each purpose, we niether lost our kits nor went without our food.

The transport consisted of the following vehicles, distributed as shown. - - -

1 L.G.S. wagon for technical signal equipment with Firing Battery.

1 L.G.S. Wagon for Officers and battery cooks' Vehicle with Frg/Battery. - (broke down about 5th day.)

-14-

an accident had to travel with Rear Wagon Line not being strong enough when repaired for fast work.

1 Mess Cart with Rear Wagon Line-Officers' Mess and 'Heavy Kits'.
1 G.S.Wagon  Q.M. Stores )
1 G.S.Wagon  Shops       ) Rear Wagon Line
also carried looted corn and ration extras.
2 G.S.Wagons from the Main Ammunition Column solely for drawing rations.

Seeing that it would be impossible to carry on without them, the C.O. as Brigade Commander, ordered the O.C. Ammunition Column to dump the S.A.A. from these two wagons, and hand it over to the Infantry, who were only too glad to have it. Our Column was not supplying the Infantry with Ammunition so this did not interfere in any way with the real vocation of the wagons. The S.A.A. supply to Infantry was run entirely by 24th D.A.C..

Had the Cooks' vehicle not broken down, the arrangements for carrying food in event of a sudden move would have been fool proof, and the cooks could not have blundered as related.

18.    With regard to positions occupied, and cover generally:  Frequently the recognised "covered position" could not be, or was not employed.
Instead of as in A. the position was more usually as in B.

A. Normal "Covered Position".

B - Battery.
C - Crest.
V - Village
FL- Front Line
E - Enemy who are also T the Target.

B.

B becomes an open position as soon as the village is taken, but was by far the most frequently occupied.
One was able to take up far more exposed positions in this open fighting without risk than of course would be possible in stationary warfare.

The recognised "open position"i.e.engaging enemy at short range over open sights, was also successfully employed. "Semi-covered position" was used in the second position at Vermand.

Cover from view when not firing, especially overhead cover, was far more important, and a hedgerow, or line of willows in the open was quite a good position to take up.

We had one good position in a yard of a house in CHAULNES, but, on the whole, villages were to be avoided as they drew fire, when the situation was uncertain.

## SUNKEN ROADS.

Sunken roads with horses are traps, and should be avoided. They give a false sense of security, but the Bosch can put shell into them, and then there is an awful mess.

Far better by day, to put horses under the lee of a bank, in a valley - if it is not too deep and narrow (which would give the same effect as a sunken road) or in the open behind a village or wood where there is room to manoeuvre or dodge. Inside a wood is alright, but nasty if suspected, and shelled, and trees start falling. On the whole, go elsewhere if possible.

Again, a line of willows or an orchard offers very good concealment, and is easy to clear out of if strafed.

The proximity of water is, of course, an important consideration.

All this is rather from the point of view of the advanced wagon line, which was of course always more exposed. The Rear Wagon Line considered comfort more than protection which they were in a position to do being farther back and comparatively safe.

## AT NIGHT.

In a choice of evils better be bang out in the open with plenty of room to move, and go there just before dark proper, when one would not be spotted moving, returning to day cover at dawn, under cover of the mist.

The idea of this being to avoid night firing or bombing which would go naturally for villages, sunk roads, valleys, etc.

Even in stationary warfare, in a part of the line we were in where night bombing of stables, and hutments, was very bad, and the surrounding country very good - plenty of good grazing - it was found by some batteries to be an excellent measure to take the horses out at dusk and picket them out for the night with a guard. N.B.. This was in summer. They thus got a good feed, and the risk of casualties was reduced to a minimum.

## Reflections after reading through:

Would any good have been realised if we had remained longer before retiring? i.e. till enemy infantry were really close to us? It seems this depends on whether the guns are -

(a) to stop the enemy, or
(b) to cover infantry retirement.

www.ingramcontent.com/pod-product-compliance
Lightning Source LLC
Chambersburg PA
CBHW081549160426
43191CB00011B/1879